Exploring
the
Marches and Borderlands
of Wales

The Celtic-Norman carving on an ancient font at Eardisley recalls in vivid detail the days of savage and relentless conflict between the Welsh and foreign invaders along the Marches and Borderlands of Wales.

Exploring
the
Marches and Borderlands
of Wales

W. T. Barber

ALAN SUTTON
1984

Alan Sutton Publishing Limited
Brunswick Road · Gloucester

First published 1984

BRITISH LIBRARY CATALOGUING IN PUBLICATION DATA

Barber, W.T.
    Exploring the Marches and borderlands of Wales.
    1.   Borders of Wales—Description and travel
    —Guide-books
    I.   Title
    914.24   DA740.B7

    ISBN 0-86299-166-8

*To my wife
in fond remembrance of her
companionship on my frequent travels
through this beautiful and historic
land of Wales*

Cover photographs and maps by W.T. Barber.
(Front) View of Ludlow from Whitcliff
(Rear) Gateway to Stokesay Castle
Photoset Linotron Palatino 10/12 by
Alan Sutton Publishing Limited.
Printed in Great Britain.

Contents

All photographs used in this book are by the author

Acknowledgements

Acknowledgements and thanks to the many people who have helped me, directly and indirectly, in collecting material for this book.

To kind people in all parts of Wales and the borderlands east of Offa's Dyke who allowed me complete access to private lands and buildings to obtain information and to take photographs.

Especially to my wife for her interest and company on my various travels, and also to other 'good companions' who were prepared to 'stand and stare' with me.

To my son Chris for reading the manuscript and for his many helpful suggestions.

* * * * * * * *

Author's Note

Maps

Sketch maps prepared by the author are placed at the beginning of each chapter, indicating the route taken and most of the towns and places visited and written about. These are a guide only and are not drawn to scale.

If more detailed information is required the Bartholomew's National Map Series: Scale 1:100 000, will be found useful. They are Maps 13, 18, 23 and 28.

The above clear and easy-to-read maps of Wales and the borderlands have also been published in book-form by Hamlyn. The scale of 1.6 miles to 1 inch, (1:100 000) enable the maps to be very detailed, and there is a most useful index. Walkers will find the relevant Ordnance Survey maps particularly useful.

Legends on Maps

Castles   ■

Churches and Abbeys etc.   ♦

Historic houses and inns.   ⌂

Roman sites   ⊠

Prehistoric sites. (Hillforts etc) ∴

Viewpoints   ✳

The Marches and
Borderlands of Wales

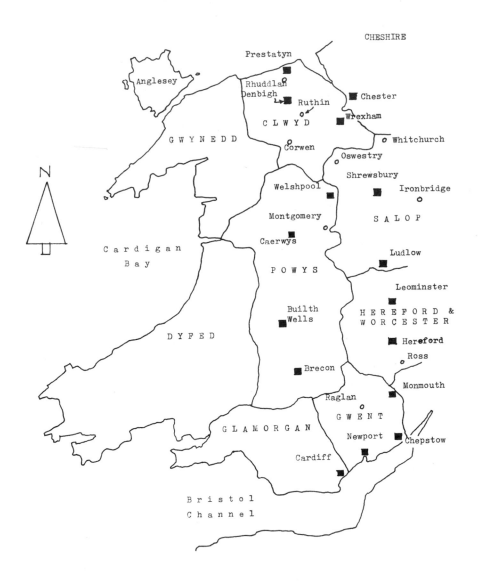

Introduction
An Historical Survey

The turbulent history of the Marches and borderland of Wales commenced long before the Roman Conquest. The story began at the time our land was joined to the Continent, and inhabited by people who set up their forts and settlements on high hills above the dank well forested valleys. During this period of prehistory successive waves of invaders came from different parts of Europe. Among them were small dark men who came from the Western Mediterranean, and during the Iron Age from Central Europe came the Celts, tall and of fair complexion.

The Celts were skilled in working metal and waging war, fearing only their priests who set up their altars of sacrifice in the centre of groves. These Druids, as recorded by Tacitus, . . . *'smeared their altars with blood from their prisoners, and sought the will of the gods by exploring the entrails of men'*. The Celtic tribes who settled in southern Wales became known as the Silures.

When Caesar led a punitive expedition to Britain in 55 BC he called all the inhabitants Britons, and wrote in his journal *'Veni, Vidi! Vici'*, *'I came, I saw, I conquered'*, but this boastful claim hardly applied to Wales until about 80 AD. The first serious invasion began in 43 AD when Claudius, hungry to obtain benefit from the mineral wealth of Britain, ordered a new invasion – one which succeeded in the occupation of the southern part of Britain in less than five years. The Britons, fragmented and poorly armed, were not able to resist the might of the Roman legions. Many who escaped the Roman sword or deportation to a life of slavery went west to set up new communities amid the mountains of Wales.

After subjugating the tribes of the south-east they marched westwards to Wales. A ford near Gloucester and a ferry across the Severn from Aust was used to bring their cohorts into Wales. The Silures, proud and savage, were stubborn opponents and the Romans soon realised that Wales would be a difficult land to conquer – in fact it took them 30 years to subdue this Celtic stronghold, and almost the same length of time to secure their grip. Here, in the land beyond the Severn and the Wye, they met their fiercest resistance, and it was not until Caradoc who, after leading the Britons in south-east Britain, was defeated, that they were able to progress into Wales. To hold down the Welsh, particularly the Silures of South Wales, the 2nd Legion of 6,000 men were garrisoned at ISCA (Caerleon-on-Usk) a place which became a fortress town which was occupied by the Romans for the full term of their 300 years' occupation.

To achieve conquest they constructed a network of military roads which for long straight miles often overlaid ancient British trackways. The stones of Roman forts stood on early earthen ramparts; ancient settlements were used as temporary marching camps, and many of the tall menhirs (standing stones) of early man bear Latin inscriptions to indicate a memorial or wayside burial. In Wales one is never far from the line of a Roman road, and many of them will bring you to sites once occupied by primitive tribes, and to lonely places where the early Celtic saints set up a Christian cross or a crude daub and wattle hermitage. One of the most important roads in Wales perpetuates the name of a Welsh maid. In 383 AD, rejecting the Roman Caesar Gratianus, the legions in Britain elected their leader Magnus Maximus as Emperor. He married the daughter of a Welsh noble and made her his Empress. The *Mabinogion* tells how he found her after a long search at the castle of Aber Sain near Caernarfon. Castles were built for her all over Wales, and between them the Roman engineers built the road now marked on our present day maps as the Sarn Helen, or Elan, considered by some to be a corruption of Sarn-y-Lleng – 'The Road of the Legion'.

When the Romans constructed their military highway between ISCA (Caerleon) and DEVA (Chester) it can be accepted that this road running through the Welsh Marches was the first boundary, or line of demarcation, between England and Wales, and remained so until the Mercian King Offa dug his famous dyke between the estuaries of the rivers Severn and Dee.

After the Romans left in 410 AD, Wales, deprived of the Roman armies who protected their border and the law and order of their civil administration, the country became divided. Princes and petty chiefs fought for each other's territory, leaving the land open for new invaders. From Europe came the Saxons and Angles, and from the cold mist-ridden lands of the Nordic seas came the dragon-prowed longships to disgorge hordes of cruel warriors to plunder and burn towns and villages along the western coast from the Isle of Mona (Anglesey) in the north to St. David's in Dyfed.

These new invasions united the warring factions in Wales and England, for the people of both countries realised that to survive their only hope was to unite against a common foe. Although the Angles and Saxons had some initial success they were not able to penetrate in force further west than Oswestry – a fact appreciated by King Offa when he started to build his rampart and dyke as a defensive boundary to protect the land he had won from Welsh attack. The Welsh led by 'Rhodri the Great', and the English by Alfred of Wessex, contained the Norsemen, and an Anglo-Welsh army trounced the Danes at Buttington on the Severn. So successful was Rhodri that when he died in 877 AD he left his beloved country free and united.

Rhodri's descendants, ruling unwisely, brought disorder, but the actions of Hywel Dda, 'Hywel the Good', did much to bring back a respect for law and order in Wales. Although this was a period when Christianity flourished and Celtic saints set up many churches, after Hywel's death the land was again disturbed by internal strife, and for personal gain many were only too ready to accept Anglo-Saxon rulers as overlords until Llywelyn ap Seisyllt ruled the land. About seventeen years after he had restored order Llywelyn was murdered in 1083 AD by jealous rivals, but his son Gruffydd proved his valour by defeating a Mercian army on the bank of the Severn at Rhyd-y-Groes, and followed this up by driving the Saxons out of Hereford.

Between 1062 and 1066 AD Wales had a foretaste of a coming struggle to retain their land which was to continue for many centuries. In the winter of 1062 King Harold invaded North Wales. The following year he turned his attentions to South Wales, but soon had to force-march his army back to south-east England to stem an invasion from across the English Channel. When defeated in 1066 by Duke William of Normandy at Hastings he opened the floodgates to an era which brought further and long-lasting trouble to Wales.

After victory at Hastings the Norman Conqueror and his followers were fully occupied in consolidating their gains, so Wales was left in peace. When the Norman warlords started quarreling with each other and harassing their leader with claims for larger rewards and seniority of position, William, a shrewd man, evolved a scheme which would keep his barons occupied and also extend his domain into Wales. He set loose his 'dogs-of-war', the Marcher Lords, to roam at will with their private armies along the borderland of Wales, and so creating the 'Welsh Marches', a term which describes the broad strip of land on each side of the border, extending from the mouth of the Wye at Chepstow to the Dee Estuary.

Like the Romans they found that it was no walk-over, and the wooden palisades they hurriedly erected, many on Welsh mounds, had to be replaced or repaired many times before it became possible for them to build more permanent keeps of stone. As always the Welsh made use of their ancient hilltop fortresses of earth and stone, and there was no more impregnable keep than a Welsh mountain. The most cruel and rapacious barons were sent to carve out their petty kingdoms, linking them to form a *march* or dividing line between England and Wales – a line which, because of Welsh resistance, advanced and receded.

Three salient points along the march were established. To Chester the Conqueror sent his nephew, Hugh of Averanche, one whose cruelty earned him the title of 'Hugh the Wolf'. A former Regent of Normandy took the title of Roger de Montgomery, and he was posted to control the Middle Marches from Shrewsbury, and to Hereford came William FitzOsbern to subjugate the southern Marches and prepare plans for the conquest of South Wales. FitzOsbern built the first *stone* castle in Wales on a high cliff above the Wye at Chepstow, and also motte and bailey castles at Ewyas Harold, Clifford and Wigmore in Herefordshire, all places visited and described in this book.

Castles were erected at intervals along the border between Chepstow and Chester. At first, sometimes on the site of prehistoric or early Celtic foundations, the Lord Marcher raised a wooden tower on a mound, and below it he created a courtyard or bailey surrounded by a strong wooden palisade. In time the wooden tower was replaced with a stone keep of immense strength, and the outer wooden walls were also replaced with ones of stone, often reinforced with a gatehouse and several towers. Around the walls of this Norman citadel would grow a town. These foreign invaders made their own laws and had the power of granting life or death; they gained possession by force of arms, or often by marriage to a Welsh heiress.

There was rarely a long period of peace in the Welsh Marches, but after bringing order to Wales Llywelyn the Great of Gwynedd formed a Council to which he summoned the native princes and Norman lords to reach agreement for a lasting peace. To further this aim he encouraged his people to form ties by marriage to Norman families. One of his daughters married a Mortimer, and another a De Braose. His own marriage to King John's daughter Joan brought him little joy, for she turned out to be as treacherous as her father when she betrayed her Welsh husband by having a torrid love affair with a Norman noble. Llywelyn gained great advantages for the Welsh when, with King John's barons, he signed the Magna Carta – but there was little hope of a just and continuous peace, so taking up arms again he took practically every castle in Wales. The famous Welsh ruler died in 1240, and his stone coffin can be seen in the Gwydir Chapel at Llanrwst.

His grandson, Llywelyn the Last, continued the fight until forced to sign a Treaty with Edward 1st at Rhuddlan in 1277. It was an uneasy peace, for he soon continued the fight to throw off the Norman yoke, always resisting the despotic tyranny of the King and his Marcher Lords. He rode to South Wales to encourage his supporters, but was slain in an obscure skirmish near Builth Wells on the 11th December 1282. Llywelyn, the *last* Welsh Prince of Wales, was soon to be replaced by the *first* English Prince of Wales, one who Edward 1st promised could not speak a word of English. Making good his promise Edward presented his newly born son to the people of Wales at Caernarfon Castle.

Many brave Welshmen continued the fight to expel the foreign invaders from their country, but after the death of the last Llywelyn one name stands out above all others – this was Owain Glyndwr who raised the standard of the Red dragon and was recognised by his countrymen as the rightful ruler of Wales. Glyndwr, a descendant of the princes of Powys, at first was friendly to English causes, fighting with Bolingbroke and with Richard II in Ireland, but when Lord Grey of Ruthin plotted to discredit him with Henry IV, causing his lands to be confiscated, his attack on Grey's stronghold at Ruthin was the signal for a Welsh revolt.

This happened in 1400, and by 1402 he established a Welsh Parliament at Machynlleth, and soon became the ruler of all Wales. In 1407 his luck ran out, his power waning after his armies were defeated by Prince Hal of Monmouth at Grosmont in Gwent and again at Pwll Melyn near Usk in Gwent. Although he was now a fugitive and outlaw not one of his countrymen would betray him to his enemies. After the capture of his wife and family at Harlech Castle, Owain, tired and dispirited, sought refuge amid his beloved mountains. He was a broken man and, according to tradition, died at the end of 1416 at the home of one of his daughters alongside the Wye near Hereford.

From then on the Welsh were second-class citizens and, in general, remained so until the start of a new era when a young Welsh squire won the heart of the widow of an English king. History is uncertain whether they were married or not, but King Henry VI recognised Owen Tudor's sons as having royal connections. When Owen lost his head on the block, a head which was 'wont to lie in a queen's lap', his followers sent his son off to Brittany. When Henry returned to Wales in 1485 the Welsh nobility and archers helped him to take the crown from Richard III at Bosworth. For the Welsh this was a glorious victory, and at last it was felt that England and Wales were really united.

Two dates are important in Welsh history, 1461 and 1485. In 1461, after winning the battle of Mortimer's Cross, Edward Mortimer became Edward IV. He curtailed the power of the Lords Marchers, decreeing that all border disputes were to be settled at the 'Court of the President and Council of Wales'. The Court was held at Ludlow, the most important town along the Welsh border. In all parts of Wales further benefit was gained in 1485 when the young Henry Tudor became King of England after defeating Richard III at Bosworth Field. The victorious Welshman refused to share power with the barons and made further curtailment. The Marcher Lords lost most of their prerogatives when Henry VIII passed a law in 1536 to merge the lordships, which had existed from the time of William the Conqueror, into five newly created counties – Denbigh, Radnor, Montgomery, Brecon and Monmouthshire. Peace now came to the border people, and the Council survived only as an administrative body until it was finally abolished in 1689.

With unavoidable omissions this is a brief history from the dim ages when Neanderthal man sought shelter from the elements and predatory beasts in caves to the time when a young Welshman of Celtic descent sat upon the throne of England.

The Book

Describes a journey through the Celtic borderland from the Severn Estuary to the Dee, starting from Chepstow where the Wye separates Wales from England. Chepstow, on the Welsh bank of the Wye, was fought over by Romans, Saxons and Normans – all races who have left proof of their sojourn in this part of south-east Wales. From Chepstow the reader is taken through historic towns and a border country whose story stretches back for more than 2,000 years.

Along the way is found ample evidence of a cruel and turbulent past; there are the primitive settlements of early man, and the Romans and Normans built so well that proof of their activities is plentiful. The principal towns, such as Monmouth, Hereford, Ludlow and Shrewsbury, and to the end of the journey at Chester, are linked by broad highways. From these busy roads green lanes following clear streams are taken to ancient villages and churches, and here and there the reader will be brought to where he can walk amid the remains of some of the splendid abbey churches built by the Cistercians and other religious orders.

The history and geography of this Celtic borderland is inseparable, for they conjure up an exciting visual background to the ancient ways and buildings and places of beauty described in this book. One is taken through sleepy castle-dominated villages up to moorland heights with breath-taking views across green valleys with expansive vistas of cloud-shadowed hills and mountains. Along these high places are the sheep-cropped tracks of the old drovers', or more ancient tracks, aligned and signposted with prehistoric stones, will lead to chambered sepulchres where one feels that the slightest violation could disturb the spirits of the dead. On the hills are deep mysterious pools and legend haunted sites with cruel and often bloody memories.

The enjoyment of exploring an area of country is enhanced by knowledge of its historical background and people. Conjectures and theories about the past are often unreliable, but the mounds, cromlechs and stones of early man, the ruins of temples and villas of the Romans and, perhaps most of all, the gaunt ruins of the Norman castles provide convincing proof of early occupation, of cruel oppressive times and the advancement of the Christian faith. The histories of the counties along the Marches of Wales are similar – they all suffered invasion, but although constant strife caused the destruction of town and hamlet each county retains a rich legacy from successive civilisations.

Stories of Wales are numerous. St. David laid the foundations of a priory in the heart of the Black Mountains, and in the Vale of Tintern a Norman lord, seeking absolution from his sins, provided money for Cistercian monks to build an abbey. The siting of their castles gives a graphic illustration of the Norman advance into Wales. Old inns and manor houses have fascinating tales of hauntings and secret passages.

Legends are the spice of history, and these have been included in this book without qualms of conscience, for many, at the time of telling, which seem far-fetched have a disconcerting habit afterwards of being substantiated. Today's facts may well become tomorrow's legends, and the reverse can also be said to be true.

It can be truly claimed that Wales is a land of beauty, song and romance. For the lover of fine scenery and history it is hoped that this book will suggest where to go, and what can be seen, often relating the present to the past.

W.T. Barber.
February 1984

Between Chepstow and Monmouth

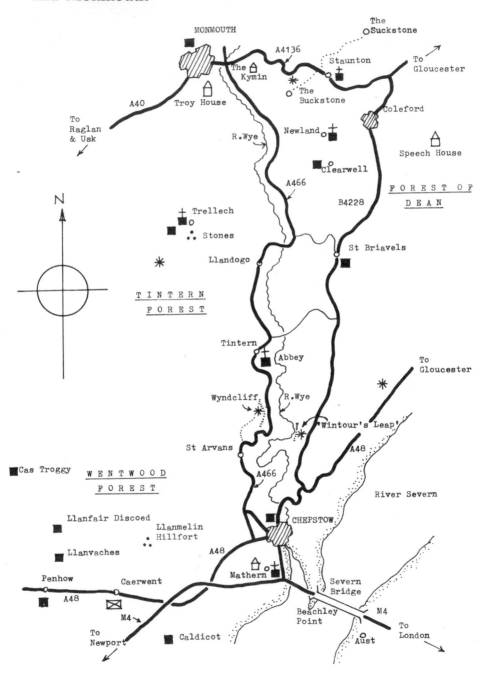

CHAPTER ONE

Between Chepstow and Monmouth

The scarred walls and battered towers of the border castles of Wales bear eloquent testimony to the tenacious opposition of the Welsh in their long struggle to defend their native land. The need to establish an inviolable boundary between the Severn Estuary and the Dee existed a long time before the Mercian King Offa constructed his ditch and rampart. Before this was done the Romans too found it necessary to maintain and garrison a long chain of forts for centuries after they had forced their way across the Severn and Wye near Chepstow.

The Celts, driven westwards through Britain, resisted the Roman advance into Wales. It took 30 years before the Romans secured their grip, but even then it was tenuous. By force of arms they occupied most of the flat borderlands but the Celts, hidden in the deep valleys and secret hollows within the mountains, never allowed them a lengthy period of undisturbed settlement, and always resisted further incursions into their beloved land.

When the Romans left to defend their homelands from the barbarian hordes the Welsh quickly realised that a land divided by tribal interests and petty feuds was a weak land, so their leaders and princes united, and when the Saxon forces crossed the border near Shrewsbury they were annihilated. Soon afterwards, in 1039, the Welsh again defeated an Anglo-Saxon army at Rhyd-y-Groes, 'the Ford of the Cross', near Welshpool, and 22 years later they opposed an army led by Harold, a king who was to open the floodgates to another invasion of Britain in 1066.

For all practical purposes the English were defeated at Hastings, but the Welsh never gave Duke William of Normandy the slightest reason to expect that they would *keep a welcome in the hills* and offer him a Welsh crown. Their valleys became wards, and the hills indomitable keeps. William sent his battle-experienced captains to probe and test the Welsh defences. One of their first points of contact was probably made where the Rivers Wye and Severn meet, just before the Severn enters the Bristol Channel. The Silures, who occupied the greater part of southern Wales, remembering stories of how their ancestors fought to prevent the Romans crossing the Wye at Chepstow, rushed down from their cliff-top fort above the river to prevent a new army led by William

FitzOsbern marching into Wales. They fought well but were no match for the trained and well-armed soldiers of the Norman war-lord who soon topped their primitive defences with a stone castle, the first of its kind in Wales.

* * * * * *

Our exploration of the English-Welsh Marches starts here. To enter Wales today entails driving down a winding hill whose name evokes memories of the past – for Castleford Hill over-lays the road which the Romans built alongside the Severn from Gloucester. Just before reaching the Wye bridge you will have your first breath-taking view of FitzOsbern's great castle, built on the edge of a high cliff above one of the loveliest rivers in Britain. Although a ruin it is still impressive, and one feels that little work is needed to restore it to its original state – a state strong enough to resist any new invasion from across the Wye.

In Saxon times Chepstow was called Cheapenstowe, 'The Place of Trade', being recognised, as it still is, as one of the Gateways to Wales. For his help at Hastings the Conqueror appointed FitzOsbern as the Earl of Hereford. With the Wye on one side and a deep ditch on the other the Norman fortress was impregnable, and remained so until the outer wall of the ward facing the ditch was breached by gun-powder in the Civil War. When the Ironside troops burst through they were opposed by Sir Nicholas Kemeys who was defending the castle for the Crown. Outnumbered, the brave leader and his men were cut down. Admission is less hazardous today, for after paying a small fee you can enter by the 'front door'. Years before the Civil War Chepstow became a walled town. Much of the medieval walling still stands, and one of the original gatehouses still exists.

Near the castle a church was built for the Benedictine monks who were brought here from France by one of the early lords of the castle. Several extensions and alterations have robbed the building of much of its original character, but the lofty nave and multi-arched west entrance give an idea of the grand and spacious minster which stood in the 12th century. The town is full of interest; a street leading to the church is flanked with picturesque almshouses, and other streets have old coaching inns. In the 18th century the town had a busy market and a port. The steep cobbled street of Hawkers' Hill was once the main coach route through the town, and at the bottom of this narrow little street you can see the unusual sign of the Five Alls Inn. On it are painted five portraits, each having its own proclamation,

Chepstow Castle and River Wye. The Norman fortress on a cliff above the Wye commands the river crossing and the entry from England into Wales.

A deep ditch, known as 'the Dell' protects the town side of the Norman castle at Chepstow.

The Soldier,	'I fight for all'
The Parson,	'I pray for all'
The King,	'I rule all'
The Lawyer,	'I plead for all'
John Bull,	'I pay for all'

Sometimes the landlord has different ideas, ordering the artist to replace one of the above with a portrait of the Devil, adding the words '*I take all*'

South of the town the River Severn is crossed by a modern suspension bridge, replacing the ferry service that once provided a crossing. The Romans called the ferry Tratica Augustus, and during the Civil War another ferry was used by Charles I when fleeing from a troop of Cromwell's men. After taking Charles across the river the loyal ferry-men returning to the Welsh coast were forced by the king's enemies to take them across the Severn in pursuit of the king. Mist now enveloped the river and the loyal men, persuading the soldiers that they had reached the English side, landed them on a rocky reef. They were left there and when the tide came up they were swept away. After this Cromwell banned the ferry which was not used again for 100 years.

West of Chepstow the flat land between the Severn Estuary and the M4 motorway contains several interesting places. At Mathern is Moynes Court, a Tudor mansion protected by a strong gatehouse, and across the fields is Mathern Palace which dates back to 1608. It was once used by the Bishops of Llandaff as an episcopal palace-home. Both houses are privately owned. In the 19th century a bishop discovered a stone coffin which he declared to contain the bones of St Tewdric, King of Glamorgan. An inscribed plaque inside Mathern church conjures up a vivid picture of what happened so many centuries ago. It is worth printing in full. It reads,

> Here Lyeth Intomb'd the Body of Theodrick, King of Morganuck, or Glamorgan. Commonly called St Thewdrick, and accounted a Martyr because he was Slain in a Battle against the Saxons being then Pagans, and in Defence of the Chriftian Religion, the Battle was fought at Tintern where he Obtained a great Victory. He died Here being in his way homward Three Days after the Battle, having taken Order with Maurice his fon Who Succeeded him in the Kingdom, that in the same place he fhould happen to Decease A Church should be built and his Body buried in ye same wich was accordingly performed in the Year 600.

The above is written exactly as set out on the plaque.

A few miles away is the large castle of Caldicot which dates back to the

The picturesque almshouses in Church Street, Chepstow, provided by Sir Walter Montagu, have been restored, but care was taken to preserve the original outline.

13th century; it was a home for the greatest Norman lords, and kings were their visitors. It stands near the site where King Harold tried to build, but his castle was destroyed by the Welsh before completion. With strong forces at Chepstow and Caldicot the Norman aristocracy felt secure from attack by the Welsh of this area, but as an extra precaution they made sure that other homes they built here could withstand hostile action. Six fortified mansions were built – at Dinham, Llanfaches, Llanfair Discoed, Castroggy, Pencoed and Penhow. Except for the latter there is little to see. Penhow Castle, on a knoll above the A48 road between Chepstow and Newport, was the first home in Britain of the great Seymour family. It is an outstanding example of a knight's castle on the Welsh border, well restored to present an accurate picture of life from the 12th to the 19th century. It is open to the public and quite easy to find.

Nearer to Chepstow is Caerwent, the Roman Venta Silurum, the only civil town they built in Wales. Near the church a notice board displays a brief written history. It reads,

> VENTA SILURUM – 'The Market Town of the Silures', a tribe whose pacification had cost the Romans 25 years fighting.
> With the end of Roman rule the town fell into decay. It became the site of a small monastery built by the Irish St Tathan, and later of a small Norman castle, the mound of which is visible in the south-east corner of the town.

Establishing a fortress at Caerleon enabled the invaders to complete the walled city of Caerwent which became one of the main centres of the Roman Empire in Britain. In time villas and civic buildings replaced the original military quarters. Rich merchants built houses within the city's massive walls, and their Silurian slaves laboured to replenish the furnaces which sent heat through the under-floor hypocausts. It is possible that ships sailed from the Severn along a widened Nedern Brook to quays alongside the walls, bringing essential goods and gossip of the latest happenings in Rome. Almost all of the immense outer walls and gateways remain, and there can still be seen the lower stone courses of villas and other buildings.

The logical starting point for a journey through the Celtic borderlands is Chepstow which is near the southern end of Offa's Dyke. Going through the archway of the medieval gatehouse a righthand turning into Welch Street will set you on your way through one of the most beautiful valleys in Britain. After St Arvans road and river twist their way between great cliffs, their rugged tops softened by a hanging cascade of greenery. Near St Arvans a track winds a cool way through woods to the top of the Wyndcliff, but a few miles further down the valley is a more

Moynes Court, Mathern. View of the splendid Tudor mansion through the gatehouse archway.

exciting ascent along narrow winding paths and up hundreds of steps.

From the high viewpoint there is an enchanting view of woodlands, and the River Wye curves in great loops past Lancaut cliffs and Chepstow Castle to join the Severn Sea. The Forest of Dean dominates the eastern horizon, and from a *gaer* behind Wyndcliff the blue cloud-shadowed Black Mountains of Gwent and Powys are seen. Across the Wye are the high cliffs of 'Wintour's Leap' where Sir John Wintour, pursued by Roundhead soldiers, dared to jump his horse from the cliff which now bears his name. It is claimed that he made a safe landing. Perhaps this story *is* true, for who can be sure – for most legends are based on some facts, even if in later years they are embellished in the telling.

Another legend claims that Tintern Abbey in the heart of the Wye Valley owes its origin to an act of penitence when Walter de Clare, Lord of Chepstow, haunted by the ghost of his wife whom he had murdered, for the salvation of his soul laid down the foundations of the abbey. He invited the Cistercians, who were also building an abbey at Neath in south Glamorgan, to help him, but this first abbey could not compare with the magnificence of the one to follow. In 1270, a descendant of the penitent Walter, Roger Bigod, Earl of Norfolk, initiated the erection of a larger building, and within 20 years enough was built for a mass to be celebrated at the altar. Patronised by kings and nobles the Cistercians prospered, achieving a state of prosperity enough to prompt Henry VIII to send his commissioners in 1537 to strip them of their riches, and even the lead from the abbey roofs. Although a ruin the building is still impressive and beautiful.

The Wye between Chepstow and Monmouth is a natural boundary between England and Wales, so why Offa ran his dyke along a ridge above the river is difficult to understand. Perhaps an additional barrier to keep out the Welsh was considered necessary or, for prestigious reasons, he wished his man-made barrier to run continuously from the Dee in the north to the Severn in the south.

There are interesting places on both sides of the dyke. From Tintern a road leads to Trellech with its three mysteries. Trellech, 'the City of the Stones', takes its name from the three monoliths which provide the first mystery. They are known as 'Harold's Stones', set up to commemorate his victory over the Britons, but it is certain that they stood here a long time before Harold was born. Their alignment precludes any theory that they once formed part of a Druidical circle, although their phallic outline suggests that they might have been ceremonial stones, revered and used by the ancients in rites of fertility. Near the stones is the second mystery – a stone enclosed well with miraculously curative water; dedicated to St Anne, it is known as 'the Virtuous Well'. The third mystery is a great mound 15ft to 20ft high and almost 400ft in circumference. The interior

Penhow Castle, the first home in Britain of the Seymours, the ancestors of a Queen of England. It is an outstanding example of a Norman border stronghold.

has never been explored, so the theory that it is the burial place of King Harold's men who were slain in battle has never been tested; it is more likely that the mound once supported a Norman keep built by the De Clare's who held other castles and estates in this part of Wales.

From Trellech a lane winds past old cottages back to the Wye Valley and the village of Llandogo. Here the Sloop Inn is a reminder that the Wye tide rose high enough to once bestow Llandogo with the prestige of being a port. From the quay ships laden with corn, cider, timber and other merchandise sailed to Chepstow, and then across the Bristol Channel to ports along the coast of Somerset (Avon) and north Devon. A reminder of those days is an old quayside pub at Bristol called the Llandogo Trow, renamed the Spyglass Inn in Stevenson's *Treasure Island*. Further along the valley is Bigsweir where a bridge crosses the Wye from Wales to England, although one is not in England until the dyke of Offa has been breached a short way along the road to Newlands and Clearwell in the Forest of Dean. Soon the road swings south to climb up to St Briavels.

If Welsh, and you had been caught near here centuries ago you would have been thrown over the ramparts of Offa's Dyke minus your sword-arm, but if caught with a forest deer you would have been thrown into the cold slimy dungeon of St Briavels Castle. There, with little sleep or food, to await a bogus trial, followed by savage punishment if not execution. In the 12th century the castle served to protect the land along the ridgeway between the Wye and Severn rivers from Welsh incursion. Here was a Royal Chase, but although game was plentiful it was not shared with the common people, and the castle was used as a court and prison for the enforcement of the forest laws. A stay at the castle today is not a prelude to a painful ordeal, for now it is a Youth Hostel where young people of all nationalities are made welcome. Centuries ago folk kept well away from St Briavels, but times are now more charitable, for every Whit-Sunday a ceremony is enacted when bread and cheese is given to the local people, marking their right to cut firewood in prescribed parts of the forest.

Coleford, in the heart of the forest, is a busy little town at the centre of several roads, a fact which justifies it being called 'the Capital of the Forest'. The town became important after it was granted a charter by Charles II for the kindness and shelter his father received after the Battle of Edgehill. A few miles away, surrounded by great oaks, is Speech House. Years ago it was a Court where the forest Verderers administered justice and settled the disputes of the foresters. It is now a comfortable hotel.

Four miles away from Coleford is Newland. If St Briavels and Speech House dealt with the secular needs of the forest people the lovely church at Newland offered spiritual comfort and guidance. The church was

The River Wye winds through the wooded valley at Tintern. View towards Llandogo from Tintern.

founded in the reign of King John by Robert of Wakering, and he was followed by priests who paid prominent parts in ecclesiastical history. One, Walter Giffard, became Archbishop of York; another, who was too ready in exclaiming views contrary to those held by exalted persons in high places, was twice excommunicated, and even imprisoned in the Tower of London.

After crossing the Severn the Romans prospected the forest for traces of precious minerals, and their workings and roads can still be seen in different parts of the forest. Coal mining began in the 13th century, and when this industry was nationalised the miners of the forest retained their freedom to work in accordance with laws recorded more than 600 years before. Inside the church is the 'Miner's Brass' which is inserted in a memorial to Sir Robert Greyndour and his wife. In 14th century clothing the miner stands on a medieval helm, a hod on his shoulder, a pick in his right hand, and in his mouth a candle-holder. Another memorial inside the church shows 15th century Jenkyn Wyrall in forester's uniform with his dog, horn and hunting knives. The memorial stone is inscribed,

> Here lythe Jun Wyrall Forester of Fee wich
> dysesyd on the VIII of Synt Lauroc the
> yeare of oure Lord MCCCCLVII on hys soule
> God have Mercie.
> Amen

Rich men build their high towered Follies from which they boast of how many counties they can see. Above the village of Staunton is a natural viewpoint overlooking the counties of Gwent, Gloucestershire, Hereford and the Forest of Dean, and also the Black Mountains beyond Abergavenny. The viewing platform is the base of an inverted pyramid of rock weighing more than 40 tons. The platform is firm and steady, but until 1885 it was a rocking stone until six foolish men from Monmouth toppled it from its perch. In time the stone, marked on the map as the Buckstone, was raised back to its original position and set in concrete so that it no longer rocks. North of Staunton, in woodland between the village and a great loop of the River Wye, is an even larger stone; this one is known as the Suckstone, and weighing about 100 tons it must be one of the largest stones in Britain.

From Staunton the A4136 road to Monmouth twists a way along the lower slope of Kymin Hill. Soon after leaving Staunton a lane on the left leads to the summit of the Kymin where a small pavilion commemorates the brave deeds of British admirals. In 1802, just two years after it was built, Britain's greatest admiral, Lord Nelson, climbed the Kymin from Monmouth to breakfast there. He was pleased to see the names of 16

The Gatehouse of St. Briavels Castle. Built on a high ridgeway between the Wye and Severn rivers the castle was once used as a Court of Justice and a prison, but is now a Youth Hostel.

fellow admirals inscribed on the memorial, and the dates of the sea battles which they had won. Lord Nelson remarked that 'Monmouth was unique in possessing the only Naval memorial (at that time) in the Kingdom'. His lordship also noted that the pavilion was dedicated to the Duchess of Beaufort, Admiral Boscawen's daughter. In slightly less than two miles the road from the top of the Kymin meets the Wye Valley road just before it crosses the river on the eastern side of Monmouth – the end of this journey.

CHAPTER TWO

From Monmouth to Ross-on-Wye

For many years the people of England and Wales were not able to agree on the national ownership of the County of Monmouthshire. Being on the Welsh side of the Wye, and of Offa's Dyke, the Welsh claimed that it belonged to Wales, but the English supported the edict of Henry VIII which, in 1553, ruled that he had annexed the county as part of his domain, and that the most important town within its boundaries supplied the county name. The Welsh, however, never accepted his decree, especially as it was made by a king who was a descendant of the first Welsh King of England. Matters have now been cleared up so that Monmouthshire, now called Gwent, *is* in Wales, and the county town of Monmouth is one where once the people wore leeks in their Monmouth caps. It is also remembered that Henry V was certain that his birthplace *was* in Wales, for he licensed his favourite squire, David Gam, to collect money in the lordship of *Monmouth in Wales* for payment of a ransom to Owain Glyndwr who had captured and imprisoned his Welsh friend and squire.

The town of Monmouth on the route of a Roman road was called Blestium. In later years it was fought for by others who tried to take this part of Gwent from a people who would never accept defeat in a battle as final, for if they lost one battle they still felt certain that in the end they would win the war. Peace here must have been established after the Normans built a castle and a priory on a high ridge between the rivers Wye and Monnow, and in time a medieval town spread round them.

Entrance from the south is through the arch of a gateway which rises from the centre of a bridge. In building this the Normans made sure that unwelcome visitors could not surprise them. It has served as a barrier for many centuries, for even as late as 1839 pierced loopholes in the stout walls supported the heavy muskets of the soldiers sent there to prevent Chartist rebels entering the town. The district south of the River Monnow and the ancient gated bridge is known as Over Monnow, and at one time a ditch called Clawdd Du encircled the area which is claimed to be the Blestium of the Romans. Over Monnow was once known as 'the Capper's Town', for here an industry thrived that brought fame and prosperity to Monmouth. The poor people of the town must have

From Monmouth to Ross-on-Wye

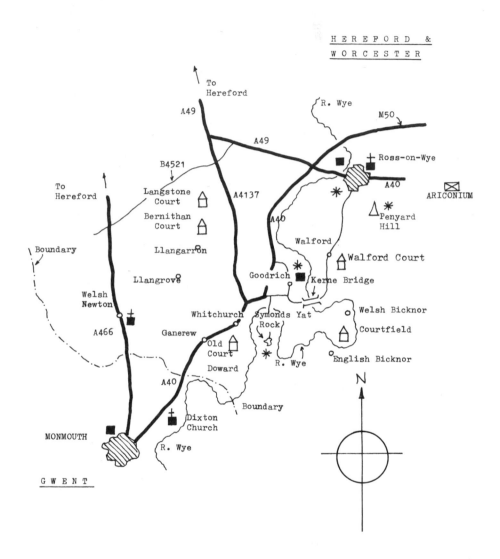

blessed Queen Elizabeth I for issuing a decree that all her commoners must wear a cap on Sundays and Holy days, and the finest ones were made by the cappers of Over Monnow. The caps became famous, especially those worn by the Welsh bowmen who helped Henry V win the Battle of Agincourt.

Go through the Norman gateway and you enter Monnow Street, a long wide highway through the centre of the town. Here and there you will find old doorways and archways of Tudor days, or a well proportioned Georgian house now used as a surgery or a small bank. Through narrow passages you will step into old world courts from which cobbled alleys end on the banks of the Wye or Monnow. On the righthand side of the street, just above the entrance to the cattle market, is the Robin Hood, one of the oldest inns in the town, and one with a secret chapel which was used in the days when it was unlawful to carry out the rites of Catholic worship. At the top of Monnow Street is Agincourt Square, so named to remind one of an English victory on a French battlefield. The English leader, Henry V, was born here in Monmouth castle and his ill-formed effigy is seen in a niche of the Shire Hall. He looks down on the statue of another famous son of Gwent – the Hon C.S. Rolls, one of the designers of a famous car, and a pioneer of aviation. Several old inns stand close to the Shire Hall; one is the Beaufort Arms where Lord Nelson stayed when he visited the town, and in the bar of the King's Head is another royal likeness, this, modelled in plaster, is of Charles I, so Monmouth can rightly claim to be a royal town.

A short lane runs from Agincourt Square to the ruins of the castle where Prince Hal of Monmouth was born. From the square you can walk through Priory Street where a small museum contains many interesting relics associated with Lord Nelson. Across the Monnow is Castle Field where, in 1233, the Battle of Monmouth was fought. Priory Street runs past a late 15th century building which once formed part of the priory where Geoffrey of Monmouth was born, and a window at first floor level is known as 'Geoffrey's Window', for he is supposed to have sat there when writing his *History of Britain*. As the historian lived 300 years earlier than the date of the present building this supposition is incorrect.

Just beyond the Nelson Museum are crossroads, the A466 running due north to Hereford, and the A40 following the river to Ross-on-Wye. Having followed the Wye from Chepstow it is logical to follow this river, the natural boundary between Wales and England, on to Ross. Less than half a mile away is Dixton where the small church of St Peter stands on an ancient riverside site where a *llan*, or enclosure, once surrounded the early Christian hermitage of Didwg. Little is known of Didwg, or the sanctuary which replaced his hermitage. It is thought that a church

St. Peter's Church at Dixton. A picturesque riverside church built in the llan *where an early Celtic saint had his hermitage.*

Langstone Court, a charming house with a gruesome story. It dates back to the 16th century.

stood here before the Conquest, for the type of masonry in the north wall of the present church suggests that it was rebuilt by the Normans as soon as they drove the Welsh away from this part of Gwent. In 1300 the officiating priest was appointed Bishop of Geneva, and about 50 years later the parish was served by a French priest, an arrangement not favoured by the Bishop of Hereford who was head of this Diocese at that time. Being so close to the river the church has been flooded many times; brass plates on the wall showing the height of recent floods.

Not far away is Ganarew, a small place squeezed between the hillside and Little Doward. On the Doward our ancestors built a camp on a site giving views of the river valley as far as Monmouth, and between the Wye and Symonds Yat to the Forest of Dean. Close to Ganarew church is a 16th century house built on the foundations of one which existed 300 years before. The present house is reputed to be haunted by someone who, according to his style of dress, lived here in Stuart times. Now and then he is seen coming down the staircase, and after pausing in the hall the ghost walks through the main entrance to vanish in the adjacent churchyard. There is no known legend to account for the sporadic visitations of the phantom.

Next along the A40 is Whitchurch, once a favourite place with the ale-tasters of Gwent in the days when Sunday drinking in their county was illegal, for here was the first pub across the English border. From Whitchurch a lane leads to an interesting hinterland lying between the A40 Ross road and the A466 Monmouth to Hereford road. In 1912 the village of Llangarron, almost central in this tract of land, hit the headlines when a number of urns were dug up near a stretch of Roman roadway. The urns contained 3,000 Roman coins; 600 were given to the British Museum and the rest were sent for safe-keeping to Hereford Museum. From other finds it is deduced that there must have been considerable Roman activity here.

Near Llangarron are two interesting 17th century houses – Bernithan Court and Langstone Court. A gruesome story is connected with the latter, one which Edgar Allen Poe could have used when writing his *Tales of Mystery and Imagination*. Some years ago, when part of the house was being altered, a small room, hardly larger than a good size cupboard, was discovered. When the workman entered it they were horrified by what they saw. Seated at a small table was a skeleton of a man, and on the table a pack of playing cards. Near the fleshless hand of the skeleton lay a pistol, and in the yellowing skull a bullet-hole. The approximate date of this tragic happening, probably suicidal, was confirmed by the Elizabethan pattern of the playing cards, and also by a coin of the same period. What actually happened will never be known, but the tragedy is obviously connected with a story of unhappiness and despair.

At Whitchurch, a short way along the turning signposted to Symonds Yat, is the 'E' shaped mansion of Old Court. This Elizabethan mansion is now, as it has been for several years, a spacious and comfortable hotel. Built on a site close to the Wye it was once the home of General Simco, the first Governor General of Canada. It is fortunate that when the lovely old house was converted to an hotel the new owners were very careful to see that any alterations and additions they made were carried out in a sensitive manner.

On the outskirts of Whitchurch the B4229 will bring you to a point where you can cross the Wye and climb Huntsham Hill to the top of a 500 ft high spur of rock which causes the river to form a great loop. From one side of the rock is a bird's-eye view of the charming riverside village of Symonds Yat, and on the other side of the rock is an equally delightful view. Both views are world famous, and are especially beautiful when the trees display their autumn tints. The name of Symonds Yat has a nautical connotation but it has nothing to do with a seaman or a yacht; Yat is a variant of *gate*, and Symonds was a 17th century landowner in these parts. Some authorities have a favourite theory that Symonds is a corruption of Seaman, and alludes to the slaughter of the Danish forces, led by 'Eric of the Bloody Axe', when a son of King Arthur defeated them in a nearby pass which is still known, and marked on the map, as 'The Slaughter'.

Return to the river crossing and the road will take you to the ruins of Goodrich Castle, the largest and most picturesque border castle in Herefordshire. To enter it you must first deal with the present custodian of the barbican, the defensive outer work which once barred the way across the moat. Now only a small fee is required for permission to cross a stepped and cobbled causeway over the deep dry moat to the entrance. All are welcome today for there is no need to fear that molten lead and boiling oil will pour down through the apertures in the gateway arch. In turn Romans and Saxons have held this site above the Wye, for the river below the castle was forded as part of the Roman military route from Gloucester (Glevum) via Monmouth (Blestium) to Caerleon (Isca) in Gwent. A document of 1101 records that Godric Mappestone built a castle here to guard the ford left by the Romans. Throughout the ensuing centuries the castle was held by a succession of Norman Marcher Lords, but seems to have been immune from serious attack until 1644 when a long siege caused the Royalist defenders to capitulate to a large force led by Colonel Birch of Weobley.

As a base from which to explore the surrounding countryside the Ye Hostelrie Hotel at Goodrich is an excellent place in which to stay. Many years ago another, but much smaller building, offered food and rest to pilgrims on their way to Tintern Abbey in the Wye Valley and Llanthony Priory in the Black Mountains of Wales. This small *hospitum* stands next

A stepped stone causeway crosses the moat to the Gatehouse of Goodrich Castle.

to the Hostelrie, an unusual building with an external staircase rising up to the doorway of an apse-shaped rear projection. It is called Y Crwys, which probably means 'The Cross'. Above the small entrance doorway is a coat of arms exhibiting 11 birds. Dean Swift visited Goodrich, and Wordsworth, who wrote a well known poem about the Vale of Tintern, was also a visitor. When he was here in 1798 he met *the little cottage girl* whose childish beauty moved the poet to write a poem about her.

From the village a lane runs over the shoulder of Coppet Hill to the Welsh and English Bicknors, the latter Bicknor is undoubtedly in England, but because of its historical association it may once have been in Wales. Shakespeare must have thought so too when he wrote of Prince Hal saying to Ffluelen, 'I am Welsh you know good countryman'. Ffluelen agreed, saying, 'All the water in the Wye cannot wash your Majesty's Welsh blood out of your body, I can tell you that'. A conversation which supports the claim that this part of Herefordshire was once in Wales. Enclosed in a loop of the Wye is a house called Courtfield, standing on the same site as one which changed its name from Greyfield to one considered by the owners more fitting for the residence of a royal prince. King Henry V is said to have spent his early childhood there in the care of the Countess of Salisbury. In a nearby church a recumbent effigy is said to be of a lady who had been nurse to Prince Hal of Monmouth.

To reach Ross-on-Wye from Goodrich the A40 can be taken, or the Wye followed from Kerne Bridge, a route which is the more interesting one to take. With the Wye on the left and a short range of hills to the right the B4228 soon reaches Walford, a place which may once have been called Welsh Ford, yet another reminder that those who occupied the lands here were of Celtic origin. Oliver Cromwell stayed at Walford Court during the seige of Goodrich Castle, and occupied a room which is now known as 'Cromwell's Chamber'. Just before reaching Ross the road runs close to Penyard Hill where once a medieval castle overlooked the Roman settlement of Ariconium, a place on the line of the Roman road which ran through the northern tip of the Forest of Dean to Glevum, now called Gloucester.

It is said that Ross was founded from the ruins of Ariconium, becoming an Anglo-Roman town named Rose Town. Another theory of how the town received its name suggests that it is a corruption of the Welsh *rhos*, a marshy place, but the hill on which Ross is built can hardly be described as a marshland. A small settlement existed on this hill in 1016, and is mentioned in 1131 as being in the See of Hereford. The Domesday Book records Ross as being a small village of just over 100 inhabitants, but as its size increased so did its importance – a fact confirmed when Henry III granted a Charter raising it to the status of a market town, and allowing four fairs to be held there during a year.

In St. Mary's churchyard a Plague Cross records the visitation of the 'Black Death' (1635–1637), when a third of the population died.

The old Market Hall at Ross-on-Wye.

During the 15th century Ross was considered important enough to have not one but two members of Parliament, but as their upkeep was too great for the people to sustain they relinquished this honour. Up to 1635 life in Ross seems to have been pleasant and uneventful until the pestilence, known as the 'Black Death' hit the town. Records show the following figures of births and burials for the two years following 1635.

In 1635 there were 62 births and 34 burials.
In 1636 there were 46 births and 72 burials.
In 1637 there were 23 births and 315 burials.

For such a small place the number of deaths in 1637 was considerable, estimated to be a third of the total population. In St Mary's churchyard a Plague Cross recalls the burial of the victims.

On a high site above the town is St Mary's church, its finest feature being a tower topped with a slender spire, a prominent landmark for miles around. The interior is also impressive, and in the chancel is a marble tomb, the final resting place of John Kyrle, 'The Man of Ross', who was loved and respected by all. He was not born in the town, but as his birth took place the same year that Ross was stricken with the plague he was fortunate to have been born at Dymock in Gloucestershire but he spent most of his life in Ross until his death in 1724. He was always ready to help those sick and in need of material help. Writers and poets paid tribute to his kindness. Samuel Coleridge Taylor considered John to be one 'nobler than kings or king-polluted lords', and Pope wrote of him,

The Man of Ross divides the weekly bread . . .
Is any sick? The Man of Ross relieves,
Prescribes, attends, the medicine makes, and gives.

In the centre of the town is the house where he lived. It is now a chemist's shop, but it does display a sign informing the visitor that it was once the 'House of the Man of Ross'.

Adjoining the churchyard is a green parkland known as The Prospect, a viewpoint to which all visitors to Ross should go. From here the Wye can be seen swinging away in a great horseshoe bend through the meadows after passing under Wilton Bridge on its way back to Goodrich; above the south-west lowlands the mountains of the Sugar Loaf, Skirrid Fawr and the Black Mountains of Wales line the distant horizon.

In the centre of Ross an ancient building impedes the flow of modern traffic. This red sandstone Market Hall dates back to the reign of Charles II. On one face of the building the king looks down on the busy street. On another facade is carved a heart intertwined with the letters F and C,

Fishing the sunlit waters of the River Wye between Monmouth and Ross-on-Wye.

At Ross-on-Wye the parkland known as The Prospect is well named, affording a wide panoramic view over the River Wye to the distant Welsh mountains.

or the F may be an inverted L which is forked into the heart – so that the monogram reads 'Love Charles to the Heart'. John Kyrle, an ardent Royalist, had the device carved on the wall so that he might see it from the window of his home.

Ross, like other towns in the Marches, retains memories of ancient customs and strange practices. If you had lived here years ago you might have been the recipient of a Welsh *'calennig'*, an ancient symbol of fertility which originated in distant times when the pagan gods of procreation were revered and worshipped by the people of this Celtic borderland. Some historians believe that the custom of presenting this symbol – a rosy apple supported on a tripod of silvered twigs, and decorated with a sprig of holly whose prickly points pierced raisins – dates back to pre-Roman days. Then there was the weird practice to ensure that the soul of the departed would rest in eternal peace. This strange rite was known as 'sin-eating', and an account of it is contained in a book describing a Wye tour published in 1821. It tells of sin-eating in Ross as follows,

> One of them (a long leane, ugly lamentable poor rascal) lived in a cottage on the Ross Highway. The manner was, that when the Corps was brought out of the house, and layd on the Biere, a loaf of bread was brought out and delivered to the Sin Eater over the Corps, and also a mazar bowl of maple, full of beer (which he was to drink up) and sixpence in money, in consideration whereof he took upon him, ipso facto, all the sinnes of the defunct, and freed him or her from walking after they were dead.

These, and other weird stories connected with birth and death are interesting memories of the past, but it is certain that they will be remembered far less than the beauty of this lovely little town on a hill above the Wye.

CHAPTER THREE

Ross-on-Wye to Hereford
and Monmouth to Hereford

There are alternative routes from Ross-on-Wye to Hereford. The most direct, after crossing the Wye over Wilton Bridge, being the A49 which eventually joins the A413 coming from Whitchurch, and further on joining with the old coach road, the A466, from Monmouth; the latter road becoming one with the A49 at King's Thorn just south of Aconbury Hill. The Wye, being the natural boundary between Wales and England, and having followed it through the Celtic borderlands from Chepstow to Ross, this seems as good a reason as any to continue the less used riverside route to the city of Hereford. To do so we leave the A499 road to Ledbury at the northern end of Ross, taking the road signposted to Brampton Abbots, a small village which once belonged to the Abbots of Gloucester.

The church at Brampton Abbots, like St Peter's at Ross, is on a hill, and from the churchyard are expansive views over the surrounding countryside and the distant forests of Gloucestershire. The church, dedicated to St Michael, was built by the Normans, but the piers which the 11th century builders erected support work which was fashionable in the 16th century. After descending Eaton Hill, the road, with several unexpected bends, reaches the east bank of the Wye just before reaching the small hamlet with the curious name of Hole-in-the-Wall. Where the road touches the Wye the river is crossed by a miniature suspension bridge which is part of a pedestrian way to Foy.

When a visitor enquired how the hamlet of Hole-in-the-Wall got its name he was told by a local expert that it was due to a big hole in the earth wall coming down from an old Roman camp, and that the same hole was the entrance to an underground passage under the river to Igestone Farm. There are several other fanciful theories accounting for the naming of this hamlet, but the most acceptable is that the name suggests a *snug corner approached by a narrow entrance*. After squeezing through this entrance the tourist will be convinced that there could be no other reason for the hamlet's quaint name.

The narrow road, although lane would be a better classification, squeezed between the river and Perrystone Woods, soon reaches How Caple where the Wye forms a great loop as it turns to the west. About 150 years ago here was the place to come if you were afflicted with bad

45

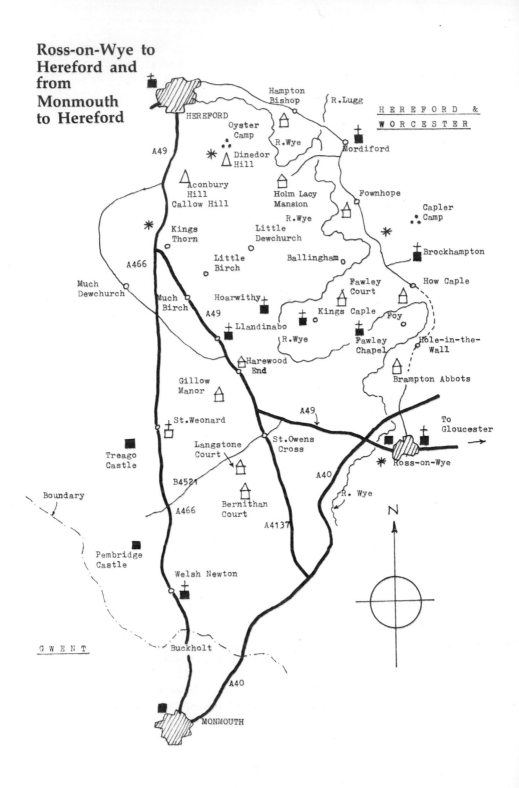

Ross-on-Wye to Hereford and from Monmouth to Hereford

HEREFORD

Hampton Bishop

R.Lugg

H E R E F O R D &
W O R C E S T E R

Oyster Camp

A49

R.Wye

Mordiford

Dinedor Hill

Aconbury Hill
Callow Hill

Holm Lacy Mansion

Fownhope

Capler Camp

R.Wye

Kings Thorn

Little Dewchurch

Brockhampton

A466

Little Birch

Ballingham

How Caple

Much Dewchurch

Much Birch

Hoarwithy

Fawley Court

A49

Kings Caple

Foy

Llandinabo

R.Wye

Fawley Chapel

Hole-in-the-Wall

Harewood End

Brampton Abbots

Gillow Manor

A49

St.Weonard

To Gloucester

Treago Castle

Langstone Court

St.Owens Cross

Ross-on-Wye

B4521

A40

R. Wye

Boundary

A466

Bernithan Court

A4137

N

Pembridge Castle

Welsh Newton

G W E N T

Buckholt

A40

MONMOUTH

eyes, for a certain cure was obtained by bathing them in water drawn from a nearby well which perpetuates the name of St Hugh. The stone mullioned windows of How Caple Court overlook the river valley, and near the house is a church with memorial windows showing the soldiers of our country from the days when they were armed with bows to more recent times when they carried a gas mask and wore a steel helmet. In another window stands a knight, and two organs are being played by a monk and an aged lady wearing an old-fashioned bonnet. A fine wooden reredos show the Last Supper, sheltered by a canopy which supports the figure of our Saviour and four attendant angels.

In almost the centre of the river loop is 16th century Fawley Court, standing with timbered outbuildings near three ponds. The piers of the entrance gates support winged beasties, two forbidding guardians of the old Court. The exact date of the house is difficult to ascertain, for front and rear facades present different architectural styles; stone in the front and timber in the rear. Such a house deserves to have its own chapel, and a short lane leads to one – a barn-like building which the Normans built on the bank of the Wye. Next along the way is King's Caple where the 14th century church is topped with a slender spire. During the 16th century the Scudamore family made a bequest to this parish church which financed the giving of Pax Cakes after the Palm Sunday service. From here the road swings back eastwards towards Brockhampton.

This river valley between Ross and Brockhampton is endowed with a richness in the style and variety of its parish churches and small manor houses. The church at Brockhampton, although a service is held there once a year, is a roofless ruin. In comparison with the grandeur of other small Herefordshire churches the new one at Brockhampton, with its thatched roof and timber belfrey has a simple and restful appearance, but is in complete harmony with the natural beauty of the surrounding countryside. Symbolical of the tranquility of this peaceful spot amid the hills of the valley is the arch-stone over the church porch carved with hovering doves. Here, too, is Brockhampton Court, an ancient house which is now an hotel.

Just after leaving Brockhampton the road rises steeply up to a matchless viewpoint between the Wye and Capler Camp. Green woods clothe the hills to north and west, and on the southward slope back to Brockhampton. Below, the river makes gracious curves through the pastureland of middle Herefordshire, and in the distance the Black Mountains cast their shadow over the land. A short climb through the woods on the right leads to Capler Camp, a 600 feet high pre-Roman fortification which, with Oyster Camp at Dinedor near Hereford, is associated with the name of the Roman General Ostorius Scapula. From the foot of the ancient camp the road makes a steep descent to Fownhope.

Fawley Court, the entrance gates guarded by two winged 'beasties'.

Brockhampton Church which has a thatched roof and several other interesting features.

When Fownhope is reached the tourist will know *exactly* where he is, for no map has such a pin-point accuracy as the old milestone which records that,

From Hereford 6¾ miles and 56 yards.
To Ross 8 miles and ⅜ yards.
To Hoarwithy Bridge 4 miles and ⅞ yards.

The sign hanging from the inn of The Green Man is just as meticulous and informative, stating that,

You travel far, you travel near,
Its here you will find the best of beer.
You pass the east, you pass the west,
If you pass this you pass the best!

The attractive inn lives up to its inviting sign, for the quality of the ale is excellent, and the interior with its half-timbered walls and brightly polished brasswork is very attractive. Village handbells hang above the bar, and an old brass-faced clock has 48 instead of the usual 60 divisions on its dial. A short way to the north is Cherry Hill supporting another encampment from which our ancestors, prehistoric and Celtic, had complete observation of the Wye ford near Holme Lacy.

Before Mordiford is reached a bridge across the Wye opposite Haugh Wood starts the way to Holme Lacy. This village took its name from the Norman Marcher Lord, Walter de Lacy, a leader appointed by William FitzOsbern to control this area after the Conquest. A tree-lined avenue leads to the mansion of Holme Lacy, one of the largest country houses in Herefordshire. In the 17th century the illustrious Scudamore family lived there. One member of this family served as an usher at the Court of King Henry VIII, and was also High Sheriff of Hereford. Another Scudamore officiated at the Court of Queen Elizabeth I, and his son was knighted for bravery in action at Cadiz, and also appointed ambassador to France. Many of the noble Scudamores lie buried in the local church. The mansion, once a comfortable Council Home for the aged and infirm of Hereford has now been closed.

Mordiford is one of the most interesting villages in this section of the Wye Valley. There are two versions of how the village got its name, but both are acceptable. Its Welsh name, Mawddwr Fford alludes to constantly flowing, or muddy, water, but if the name Rhyd-y-Morddy is preferred this would mean 'The ford of the agitated water'. The village stands on the bank of the river Lugg which, after flowing under Mordiford bridge, joins the Wye, a river which provided a fortunate overflow when the village was flooded about 165 years ago. Then, a

The Green Man of Fownhope. His threatening attitude is contradicted by the words of welcome seen on the right of the picture.

Gillow Manor, a late 14th Century fortified house partly surrounded by a moat.

tributary of the Lugg poured more water into the river than its banks could contain, so that the floodwater swept away several cottages and drowned four of the villagers. A local record states that the Lugg became 20 feet deeper and 180 feet wide.

If an old legend is true Mordiford, for another reason, was a place to avoid, for in a nearby wood the 'Mordiford Dragon' had its lair. Years ago the west wall of the church was decorated with a painting of a huge green dragon with a forked red tongue. The wall also bore an inscription stating,

> This is the true effigy of the strange
> Prodigious monster, which our woods did range,
> In Eastwood it by Garson's hand was slayne,
> A truth which old mythologists maintayne.

The green-scaled creature came down to drink where the Lugg joins the Wye, and when he did so the beast usually devoured one or more of the villagers. Mordiford had its local dragon-slayer who managed to trap the dragon and shoot an arrow through its heart, but he was so overcome by the beast's nauseous breath that he died. The way taken by the monster to reach the river is still called 'Serpent's Bane', and it is said that grass never grows on it. A local historian, not favouring this fanciful legend, suggests that the story is based on racial memories of the dragon decorated banners carried by the Danes when the Saxons met them in battle at Mordiford.

Green is a colour which seems to be associated with Mordiford. There is a carving of a 'Green Man' in Mordiford church. He has an evil expression and, with vine or oak leaves sprouting from his wide and cruel mouth, he leers down on the congregation. There is no token of welcome here, unlike the sign of 'The Green Man' over the entrance to the yard of a nearby inn which suggests hospitality and friendship to all.

The next village is Hampton Bishop, a place of half-timbered cottages and an ancient church. The road touches the Wye again when The Bunch of Carrots is reached. This attractive inn is also eager to offer a friendly greeting to the stranger, for above the entrance are the words 'Welcome ye coming; speed ye parting guest'. The inn was built in the 17th century, but subsequent alterations have been carried out with good taste, so that an extension, once a cider-mill, has been converted to a restaurant in a manner which would meet the approval of any architectural purist. Behind the inn is a salmon pool which probably supplies the restaurant with fresh salmon, and is also a favourite spot for anglers from all parts of Herefordshire. The city of Hereford is near, and from the bedroom windows of the inn you can see the tall towers and spires of the city cathedral and churches. Look westwards and you

The inn sign of Harewood End is an interesting pictorial representation of the inn's name.

can see the tree-clad summits which now surround the contours of pre-Roman encampments on Dinedor and Aconbury Hills.

* * * * * * * * * *

The direct route from Ross to Hereford is, after crossing the Wye over Wilton Bridge, along the A49 trunk road. This highway joins the A466 road from Monmouth just south of Aconbury Hill; both routes will be found interesting. After about three miles along the A49 a lane on the left leads to Gillow Manor, a late 14th century fortified home encircled by a moat. Except for a massive gatehouse and a wing which was once a chapel there is little left of the original house.

The wayside inn signs compete with each other to catch the interest of potential customers. The sign displayed at Harewood End, a mile from the turning to Gillow Manor, must have been designed by someone with a good sense of humour. The inn is called Harewood End, and the sign is a pictorial representation of its name. It shows the *rear* view of a large hare, and facing a thick *wood* he makes an eloquent display of his stubby white *tail*. HARE-WOOD-END, of course!

After another mile we reach Llandinabo with its small church dedicated to St Dinabo. Little is known of him except that he was an early Welsh saint, and may have been a cousin to St Dubricius, one of the Bishops of Llandaff. For the brass-rubbing enthusiast the church contains the quaint brass of Thomas Tomkins, standing in water and wearing a cross on a cord about his neck. Thomas was drowned in 1629. There is also one of the loveliest screens in Herefordshire; it dates from Tudor times and is richly carved with figures of dolphins, mermaids and angels. Just north of Llandinabo a lane on the right will bring you to a completely different church, one that looks out of place in an English countryside. Hoarwithy church, with its high campanile and other Italianate features would be more suitable in Italy, or among the buildings of Port Meirion in North Wales.

Further north is the small village of Little Dewchurch – in fact there are two Dewchurch's, the other, known as Much Dewchurch, lies astride the B4348 due west of the minor village. Their names perpetuate the memory of Dewi Sant (St David) supplying further evidence that this part of Herefordshire was once in Wales – particularly as Much Dewchurch was once called Llanddwei. Nearby is the old British Camp, marked on the map as Wormelow Tump, claimed by some historians to be the burial place of a man called Amwr. This seems to be an area of twin villages, for in the vicinity are Much Birch and Little Birch. Above them rises Aconbury Hill on which the ancient British dug deep ditches and mounded the excavated earth to form ramparts of a camp which covered more than 20 acres. Below this 900 feet hill is a small church which is said to stand on the site of a 13th century nunnery, founded in the reign of King John by the wife of Walter de Lacy. Perhaps the stone effigy above the porch is that of Margaret de Lacy.

The A49 now meets the old road coming from Monmouth, both roads combining to run along the west side of Aconbury Hill to the top of the Callow. To Hereford people the Callow was once considered a steep and difficult hill to climb, and one connected with strange stories of hauntings and other mysterious happenings. To follow easier contours the original route of the Callow has been altered – but if you are brave, or curious enough, to use the old way you may see at night the dark silhouette and eerie lights of a ghost house which was demolished a long time ago. From the top of the Callow you can look down and over the city of Hereford.

If you wish to avoid taking the busy, but faster, A40 motor road from Monmouth to Hereford, then the A466 is the road to take. From the outskirts of Monmouth the road follows the Monnow river for a short distance before ascending the Buckholt to reach Welsh Newton. In the churchyard here is the tomb of John Kemble, a Roman Catholic priest who was hanged at Hereford in 1679 for conducting mass at Pembridge Castle. The burial place of the 80 year old priest is marked by a simple stone inscribed 'J.K., Died the 22nd of August Anno D. 1679'. A grim reminder of those days of intolerence and persecution lies in a casket at the Roman Catholic church in Hereford. There you can see the mummified hand of the unfortunate priest. Shortly before his death John Kemble lived at Pembridge Castle, serving as a chaplain to the Scudamore family. The castle is now a private home, but 700 years ago it was the fortress of a feudal lord, and many of the features of medieval days can still be seen. Special permission is required to visit the castle.

The old Monmouth to Hereford coach road runs directly north, and after reaching the crossroads where the B4521 comes from Skenfrith in Gwent on its way to Ross-on-Wye, the village of St Weonard lies just ahead. This is the starting point for visiting another (with permission of the owner) interesting castle at Treago. Before doing so walk around St Weonard which is situated on a hill-top halfway between Monmouth and Hereford. This area seems to have been one favoured by the lesser known Welsh saints, and the village is named after one of them – St Weonard. His effigy is in the east window of a chapel where he stands in company of Our Lord and the figures of some better known saints. He holds a book and an axe, items of some unknown symbolism. His name might be a corruption of St Gwainerth, a holy man reputed to have been murdered by the marauding Saxons. It is said that he lies buried in a golden casket under some undiscovered local tumulus.

From St Weonard, after crossing the Garron Brook, you will find

Treago Castle, near Welsh Newton, stands on a site which dates back to the closing years of the 11th century.

Pembridge Castle where the martyr John Kemble served as chaplain to the Scudamore family.

Treago Castle. History is not clear about its name which implies that it was once the home of James, a person of whom there is no information. It is thought that an estate here was originally awarded to the De Minore family by the Conqueror for their services to him at Hastings, but the foundations of Treago were not laid down until the reign of King Stephen. It is interesting to learn that the present occupants of the castle are the direct descendants of the De Minores, a family of Norman origin, who first held land and some property at Burghill to the north-east of Hereford.

The author would like to record his thanks to Sir Humphrey Mynors for his kind efforts in providing a well researched and authentic history of his home. Thanks are also due to his brother, Sir Roger, for permission to wander at will inside and around the lovely gardens of this historic castle.

The careful research made suggests that many stories of the history of Treago and its owners are, if not lacking in imagination, spurious. One story is that the inner courtyard (now roofed over) was used as a stockyard when news came that Welsh raiders were about. The court was much too small for such a purpose, serving only as a light-well for the illumination of surrounding rooms. That the yard contained a well *is true* for this still exists.

Two upper rooms in the towers are of interest. The south-east tower has a handsome fireplace, and on one of the walls hang the Raphael cartoons for the Mortlake tapestries. A small room in the north-west tower, called the 'Pope's Hole', is wrongly supposed to have served as a secret hiding place for those of Papist inclination. It's easily found location in the tower precludes such an idea, but a small staircase landing nearby does have some loose boards laid over a small box-size hole which may have been such a hiding place, and one not easily detected by searchers. As the Mynors were recusants and always loyal to the Crown it is very possible that the small claustrophobic chamber was used, and also that the tower room housed travelling Roman Catholic priests.

In the 'Pope's Hole' an oil painting is claimed by some to be that of Father William Harecourt who, at the age of 70, with other Jesuit priests, was found guilty of high treason and was sentenced to death by decapitation. Whoever the picture is of (and this is uncertain) it is a gruesome one. It is of an aged man with a ribbon around his neck which barely conceals the dripping blood and, in a symbolic mood, the artist has painted an axe, a dagger and a skull. At the time of the Civil War the occupants of Treago were often in trouble for their loyalty to the Crown, but favour and peace was restored to them when Charles II regained the English throne.

Here and there are displayed sections of the huge roof trusses which supported the heavy roof above the Hall, and cabinets contain relics and dresses worn by the family in bygone days. There are several splendid family portraits; among them is that of a Governor of the East India Company, a Governor of the Bank of England, and a Lord Mayor of London, Sir Gilbert Heathcote, a man, according to Pope, not easily fooled. A couplet written by Pope reads,

> The grave Sir Gilbert
> takes it for a rule
> That every man in want is
> knave or fool

The hinterland between the A466 and the A49 coming from Ross has already been explored so except for the expansive view of the countryside of Gwent and Herefordshire, backed by the distant mountains of Wales, there is little to interest the tourist between St Weonard and the forked road junction with the A49 below Aconbury Hill from where the road runs down the Callow to Hereford.

Between the Rivers Wye and Arrow

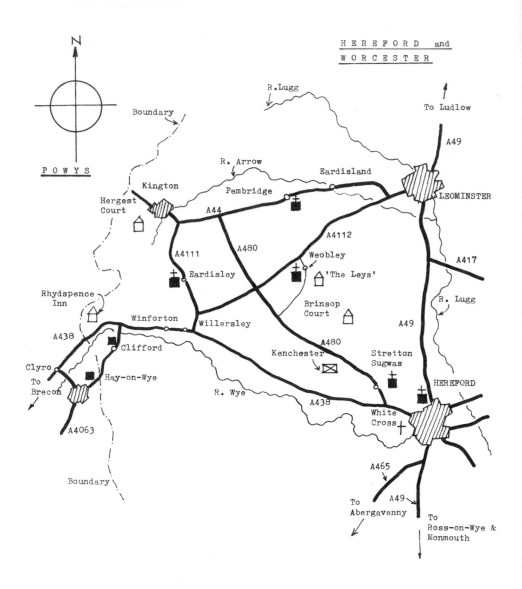

CHAPTER FOUR

Between the Rivers Wye and Arrow

Hay-on-Wye is the most convenient town from which to start exploration of the villages and countryside of north-west Herefordshire, an area between the rivers Wye and Arrow. At Hay Welsh and English once glowered angrily at each other across the Dulas Brook, and they were never slow in rustling any sheep or cattle which strayed too near the border. At one time, to keep everyone satisfied, the town was artificially divided in two – English Hay and Welsh Hay, but now it is officially recognised as being an entirely Welsh town.

Where the Normans built a castle it was sure to be a place destined to suffer interminable strife; Hay was such a place and had two castles. One, probably an early Silurian fortification, which may also have been used for a time by the Normans, is on the Welsh side of the dyke and rampart which King Offa built as an inviolable boundary between England and Wales. Indeed, if any Welshman was found on the wrong side of the dyke he was certain to lose his right arm if not his life.

The Silurian castle is near the dyke where it crosses the Wye just north of Hay; the other, a Norman castle, was built by Bernard de Newmarch in the centre of the town. For various reasons, particularly when a Norman castle-owner fell out of royal favour, a castle changed hands several times, so that the newly appointed owner often had to batter the walls to gain an entry. This may have been the case at Hay, but the castle remained fairly intact until that 'ogre of all Lord Marchers', William de Braose, fell foul of King John who marched into the town and reduced the fortress to a charred and battered ruin. De Braose managed to escape, leaving his wife to face the king. Failing to comply with the monarch's wishes she was sent to spend the rest of her life in misery and starvation in a dungeon at Windsor Castle. After being battered and burnt the castle was repaired, but 200 years later Owain Glyndwr paid it a similar compliment.

The small market town is internationally known for its bookshops, each shop specialising in new and secondhand books to suit all tastes. Even the local cinema has been converted into a multi-tiered book-store and warehouse containing thousands of books. Visitors, and they come from all parts of the world, can be reasonably certain of finding the rare volume they are searching for.

Across the Wye is Clyro, situated between the river and the foothills of an area which gave concealment to the encampments of Welsh patriots. Not far from here the treacherous De Braose committed another dark deed. Inviting a Welsh chieftain to meet him to agree settlement on some matter which was in dispute, he seized the Welshman, bound him to the tail of a horse, and dragged him to Brecon to a cruel execution.

Fighting between Norman and Welsh must have been incessant. They kept close watch on each other, the Welsh from their lairs amid the Radnorshire hills, and the Normans from the mound they threw up at Clyro which they fortified and used to guard the river crossing. From it they could monitor the river valley and any sign of the Welsh emerging from the Begwyn Hills which rise 1,000 feet above the river. Centuries before this the Romans also built a fort here, just on the Welsh side of Offa's Dyke.

Across the Wye at Clifford the ruins of another fortress rise from a small plateau above the Wye, a castle used to shelter the soldiers of William de Braose to command the upper Wye valley. After subjugation of the local partisans it was probably used as a lodge, for hunting and fishing were favourite Norman recreations. Soon after the Conquest it became the home of the Cliffords, and found fame as the birthplace of 'Fair Rosamond', the young maid who became the mistress of a King of England. Rosamond (Jane de Clifford) was not always happy about this arrangement, one certainly not favoured by Queen Eleanor whose glance was far less approving than that of her husband, King Henry II.

Along the A438 road, on the boundary between Wales and England, is the Rhydspence Inn, one of the oldest buildings in Herefordshire dating back to 1350. This half-timbered inn was once a station on the route of the Welsh drovers' taking their cattle 'on the hoof' from Wales to English markets, going even as far as Smithfield in London. The inn then was noted for its excellent cider, and the old press which manufactured the apple-juice still stands at the side of the building. Walk down to the Wye and you will stand where there was a ford which enabled the drovers' to take their cattle across the river. This ford, or to use the Welsh name, *rhyd*, is connected with the name of the inn.

There are inns where county boundaries run through the centre of the building, making it lawful for Sunday morning drinks to be served in one bar but not in another. Other pubs in Wales are separated by a river boundary, so that regular weekly customers of an inn in a 'dry' county can only quench their Sabbath thirst by crossing the river to the adjoining county where drinking is legal. Being within a few yards of the border Sunday trade at the Rhydspence is good, for it is known to be the *first* pub in England, and if a cautionary warning is necessary for the English, it is also the *last* pub in their country.

The old Rhydspence Inn is situated close to the Wye where a ford was used by the Welsh drovers to herd their cattle across the river.

Some of the picturesque 'black and white' timber framed houses of Eardisley.

When Winforton is reached suggestions of the traditional timber built buildings of Herefordshire are seen in the farm buildings with their vertical walls of planked weather-boarding. This corner of the county is sheltered from the cold north winds by the Radnorshire hills, and the Black Mountains of Wales break the full force of the south-west gales. The pastureland is rich, the soil made fertile by the gentle action of sun and rain, and there are charming villages where black and white timbered houses cluster close to historic castles and stout-towered churches. The ruined keeps of Norman castles are constant reminders that this lovely Celtic borderland was not always a peaceful place in which to live.

There are few more attractive villages in Britain than those of Eardisley, Pembridge, Eardisland and Weobley; or medieval manor houses which comapre with the moated Courts of Brinsop and Brock-hampton, and the multi-gabled manor of The Leys near Weobley. Eardisley, the first of these villages, is a quiet place with picturesque houses and an ancient church. It had its castle too, and here an unpopular bishop of the great cathedral at Hereford was imprisoned in 1262. Peter Aquablanca came to Britain with the French bride of King Henry III, and it was not long before he became Bishop of Hereford, making use of his powerful position to enrich himself and impose heavy taxes to finance his royal master's foreign adventures.

A mound now marks the site of the castle, and perhaps where an earlier motte and bailey stood. Inside the church is a relic of less peaceful times – a 15th century helm which was unearthed near the site of the castle. Several houses in the village have historical associations; one of them was used by Cromwell as a base when organising an attack on the castle. He slept in this house, but it is unlikely that he reposed in the 'Coffin Room', so called because the monks who once occupied the house were laid out in this chamber when they died. Near the church is a *long-house*, a type of dwelling more common to Wales than England. These long and low houses sheltered the family at one end and the animal stock at the other. Now, well-restored, it has been converted into three or more separate dwellings.

Inside the church is Eardisley's greatest treasure – a Norman tub shaped font, decorated by Celtic craftsmen who were more artistic and not so heavy-handed as the Norman stone carvers. The 12th century font is in a perfect state of preservation. The deeply cut carvings are similar to work at Kilpeck church, and probably done by the same craftsmen whose work can be seen in other Herefordshire churches. Warriors, unlike those carved on the south doorway at Kilpeck,* are shown in action. One brandishes a large sword, but his adversery was quicker for he has run his spear through the swordman's leg. The warriors wear pleated trousers, or trews, scarflike waistbands and pointed caps which may have inspired the design of the famous 'Monmouth caps'. Another carving shows Christ rescuing Adam, or maybe St Peter, from the jaws of a lion.

The route taken to reach the half-timbered village of Pembridge runs near Kington which, although small, claims to be a town and also the oldest in the county. If this is true then the castle near the river Arrow, with the curious Welsh sounding name of Castle Twt, must be very ancient. Two ladies of very different character are associated with Kington. One was Ellen Gethin who became known as 'Elin the Terrible'. She earned this uncomplimentary name after, dressed as a man, she went to an archery contest where she shot her brother's murderer through his heart. The other lady of Kington was the famous actress Mrs Siddons, who made her first stage appearance in a barn near the 17th century Talbot Hotel.

Not far away is Hergest Court, a place with a dark history, and tales of secret rooms and ghosts. Standing on a partly moated mound suggests that the house had seen military action. The steep ridge of Hergest rises behind the house, the hunting ground of the legendary 'Black Hound of Hergest' whose appearance foretold death. Sir Arthur Conan Doyle stayed at a nearby house, so it is quite feasible that his famous novel, *The Hound of the Baskervilles*, was founded on the legend of the ghost-hound, and also connected with the name of Baskerville, a family who once lived at Eardisley.

Lady Charlotte Guest, when compiling the Mabinogion, found a great deal of material in the *'Red Book of Hergest'* which at that time was stored at Hergest Court. This book has been described as 'a rich and varied store of Welsh literature, prose and verse', written by Welsh medieval poets; it is now in the Bodleian Library at Oxford. One of the Vaughan family who lived at Hergest had an evil reputation, so he became known as 'Black Vaughan'. Even after death he continued to haunt and trouble the neighbourhood so much that the people pleaded with the church to conduct a ceremony of exorcism to rid them of this troublesome spirit. It must have been a difficult and dangerous exorcism, for 12 of the 13 priests who conjured up Vaughan's black spirit fainted with fright. The priest who continued the ceremony was braver, and after reducing Vaughan to the size of an insect he imprisoned him in a snuff box which he then placed under a large stone at the bottom of Hergest Pool. Some years later the pool was drained and the snuff box was found. When it was opened the neighbourhood was troubled once more. After another exorcism the ghost was laid again – this time under a large tree.

Pembridge, the next place to visit, is built almost entirely of timber. Towering above the square is the detached tower of the church, a strange pagoda-like structure supported inside by a complex network of massive beams and posts, cunningly jointed and wooden pegged to

At Eardisley this typical Welsh 'long-house' may once have housed the family at one end and the animal stock at the other.

Opposite the New Inn at Pembridge, a place known for its breed of Hereford cattle, is the 500 year old timber-built market hall.

support the square dome of the belfry. Certainly a curious style of architecture to be found in Herefordshire – one which could be called '14th century pagoda'. Pembridge is obviously not a 'new town' for the medieval builders, unhampered by the foibles and dictates of present-day planners – who insist on uniformity of design and layout – have achieved harmony coupled with individuality of design and layout.

In the centre of the square is the open-plan Market Hall, its moss-covered tile roof supported by eight wooden pillars, one of which stands on the base of a cross which was here before the hall was built, and was a gathering point for early Christians. In the square is the New Inn, a tall structure with a timbered front and ornate brackets supporting the overhanging upper storeys. The original inn stood here in 1311, but if only a small part of the present inn is 14th century perhaps a name different from the present one should have been given. When a coaching inn on the road to Aberystwyth there must have been uncertain thoughts about a suitable name, for then it was referred to as 'The Inn without a Name'.

Martial sounds must have disturbed the peace of the village when an army marched through it in 1461 to a battle at Mortimer's Cross which changed the course of English history. It was a cold frosty morning when the young Duke of York led his supporters to meet the Lancastrian army headed by Owen Tudor. Historians, scientifically informed, consider the state of the weather over the battlefield to have been responsible for the freak refraction of light and ice particles for *three* suns to have appeared in the sky. Young Edward considered it a good omen, and afterwards used a symbol of three suns in his heraldic arms. The battle brought victory to the young Duke who became Edward IV of England. His head wore a crown, but the unhappy Owen Tudor lost his on the executioner's block in the centre of Hereford town.

The next village we call at is Eardisland, considered to be the prettiest one in Herefordshire, owing much of its charm to its riverside situation. The Arrow flows through the centre of the village, and near the bridge a clever arrangement of landscaping forms a tree and shrub-lined pool on which gaily plumaged waterfowl swim for the entertainment of visitors, and sometimes the placid water is rippled by the rising of a fly-hungry trout. The finest house in the village, Staick House, stands opposite the pool, and although built nearly 700 years ago it still retains much of the original timberwork, windows and large fireplaces. In the garden are trees trimmed in shape of peacocks. Two other interesting houses are also near the pool and bridge. One is the old School House, and the other is a manor house.

Any proud native of this lovely county will be certain to select Weobley as being a place which has the finest selection of traditional black and white timber buildings. The way is well signposted, particu-

Practically all of the Pembridge buildings are constructed of timber. Here are some which line the main street through the village.

As well as houses, Weobley has several fine inns – The Unicorn is one of them.

larly when you catch sight of the tall church tower with a steeple supported by flying buttresses, an unusual feature of country parish churches. Church memorials are a mine of information regarding local history, and of notable citizens. Inside Weobley church is a great deal of information, especially about Colonel Birch who lived here after the Civil War. His marble effigy is very impressive. Clad in armour he stands in a dictatorial attitude and has a facial resemblence to David Lloyd George, so it is no surprise to learn that he had been the local member of Parliament.

He was something of a wheeler-dealer, very astute and always quick to take advantage of the propitious moment. He was once a trader until his robust defence of his packhorse train so impressed Cromwell that he made him a Captain of Horse in the Ironside army. Birch prospered and soon 'acquired' episcopal palaces, manors and land. Remembering his trading days he bought lead from the roof of vandalised buildings at scandalous prices. He was certainly a man for the moment, and one to hedge his bets, for at the Restoration he decided that it was in his interest to help King Charles II. In later years, perhaps for the good of his soul, or because it was natural for him to ensure his welfare in this world and the next, he made handsome contributions to enrich the church at Weobley.

The 14th century Red Lion Inn, one of the oldest in Herefordshire, keeping the reputation the village has always had for its good ale, supports the old saying of 'Lemster (Leominster) for bread, Weobley for ale'. When King Charles I came here after the Battle of Naseby in 1645 he preferred the brew at the Crown Inn, for it was there that he stayed. To commemorate the royal patronage the pub was renamed The Throne. It is now a private house known as Throne Farm.

The Normans called the village Wibela, but smaller than it is today it was not then able to claim that it had the widest street in the county. Again, as at Pembridge, the medieval architecture is varied, competing with the beauty of the surrounding countryside of rich apple orchards and lush meadow lands. The finest example of medieval domestic architecture can be found just south-west of the village. The Leys, faithfully mirrored in a small pond, must be one of the loveliest houses in Herefordshire. James Brydges, who built the house in 1589 must have been a supporter of Cromwell, for in the attic an explicit directive was found ordering the Ironside troops not to attack or damage the house in any way, so this may account for its excellent state of preservation.

Another interesting house is the moated 14th century manor of Brinsop Court. Centuries ago access to the house was difficult, for at the first sight of unwelcome visitors a stout drawbridge was raised above the moat, and the owners quickly prepared to defend their home against borderland brigands. Inside the house great beams span the large hall to

Part of the Red Lion inn at Weobley is an example of the old 'cruck' construction.

The Leys, a silver-toned timber framed house on the outskirts of Weobley.

support the king posts of trusses jointed and pegged by medieval carpenters 600 years ago. Ancient records claim that the first owner was Ralph Tirrell, then when the property passed to the Dansy family in the 15th century it remained with them for 400 years until 1820. The poet Wordsworth and his sister Dorothy were visitors, and windows in Brinsop church honour the Lakeland poet and his family.

Next comes Bishopston, built along the Roman road to Kenchester, the Roman city of Magna Castra. A Roman villa once stood on the site of the present rectory, and when excavations for the foundations were dug mosaic floors were uncovered. Near to the site urns containing many Roman coins were also discovered. During an archaeological dig Wordsworth visited the site, and what he saw inspired him to record that,

> Fresh and clear . . . as if its hues were of the passing years,
> Comes this time-buried pavement, from the mound,
> Hoards may have come of Trajans, Maximus,
> Shrunk to coins with all their warlike toil. . .
> The casual treasures from the unfurrowed pit.

Magna Castra was built on the line of the Roman highway which ran from Caerleon (Isca) through Abergavenny (Gobannium) to Uriconium near Shewsbury. Like their city of Caerwent in Gwent this 'new town' had wide metalled streets, wine shops, a market place, baths and villas with brightly patterned mosaic floors. Overlooking the Roman site is an even older place of habitation and refuge – Credenhill Wood where trees now cast concealing shadows over the deep-cut ditches and ramparts of a British camp. This hilltop fortress must have kept the well-fed indolent citizens of Magna constantly alert. The old Roman road, marked Watling Street on the map, runs through Credenhill village to Kenchester.

Credenhill village is named from the Iron Age camp associated with the Mercian King Creda. It must have been a very difficult fort to take, so it is not easy to understand why the Romans, who were masters of military strategy, built Magna at the foot of an enemy stronghold from which they could often be attacked. It was a vulnerable spot, so perhaps they did suffer harassment from the British, and more than enough to cause them to seek a more peaceful site on the banks of the Wye at Hereford, a city whose first walls are supposed to have been built by the Romans. Another long stretch of Roman road runs in a straight line from Stretton Sugwas to Hereford.

Stretton Sugwas church is easily identified, for here the nave and sanctuary lie below an unusual half-timbered tower, a type of construction not used by the Norman church builders. Inside the church can be seen further work carried out by the Kilpeck carvers – craftsmen whose work might well have been to the approval of Picasso. Above a Norman

Eardisland is also a picturesque Herefordshire village. Staick House is a fine example of medieval workmanship.

The 600 year old Brinsop Court, often visited by the poet Wordsworth and his sister Dorothy.

doorway a stylised figure of Samson rides a lion and he is attempting to force open its jaws.

Exploration of this land between the rivers Wye and Arrow ends at Whitecross on the outskirts of Hereford where an ancient cross is a reminder that in 1361 this city was one to avoid. In that year open drainage channels and deep cess pits polluted the wells of the city, spreading through the narrow streets an 'unprecedented and out-rageous plague'. People were barred from entering or leaving, so it was arranged for food gathered from the surrounding countryside to be left for collection at Whitecross. Years afterwards a cross was erected to replace the original one which was built to commemorate the visitation of the dreadful scourge which was known as 'The Black Death'.

Between the Black Mountains and The Wye

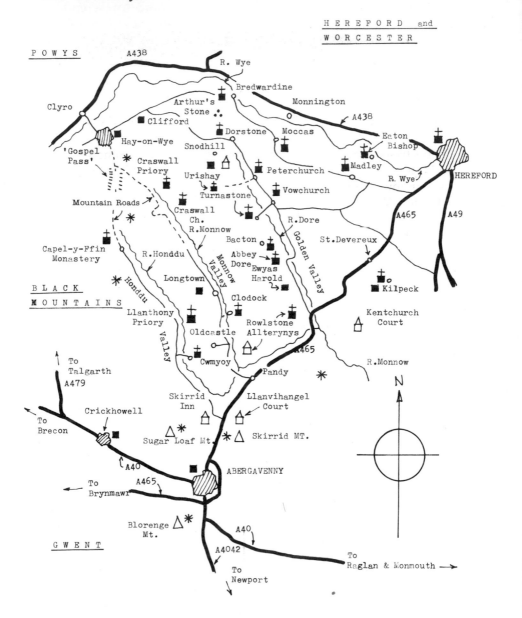

HEREFORD and WORCESTER

POWYS

A438

R. Wye

Bredwardine

Clyro

Arthur's Stone

Monnington

Clifford

A438

Dorstone

Moccas

Eaton Bishop

Hay-on-Wye

Snodhill

HEREFORD

'Gospel Pass'

Craswall Priory

Urishay

Peterchurch

Madley

R. Wye

Mountain Roads

Turnastone

Vowchurch

Craswall Ch.

R.Monnow

R.Dore

Capel-y-Ffin Monastery

R. Honddu

Bacton

St.Devereux

A465

A49

BLACK MOUNTAINS

Longtown

Monnow Valley

Abbey Dore

Ewyas Harold

Golden Valley

Kilpeck

Honddu Valley

Llanthony Priory

Clodock

Kentchurch Court

To Talgarth A479

Oldcastle

Rowlstone Allterynys

A465

Cwmyoy

R.Monnow

Pandy

To Brecon

Skirrid Inn

Llanvihangel Court

N

Crickhowell

A40

Sugar Loaf Mt.

Skirrid MT.

To Brynmawr

A465

ABERGAVENNY

Blorenge Mt.

A40

GWENT

A4042

To Raglan & Monmouth

To Newport

CHAPTER FIVE

Between the Black Mountains and the Wye

From the bleak moorland heights above the steep escarpment of the Black Mountains and the northern foothills of the land between the rivers Monnow and Wye are several river valleys. The most spectacular, the Honddu Valley, runs through the heart of the mountains from a narrow cleft in the escarpment above Hay-on-Wye. Next, running along the eastern flank of the mountains is the valley of the Monnow, the river being joined near Longtown by the Escley Brook. Further east the Dore river springs from Merbach Hill to run through the lush water-meadows of the Golden Valley to join the Monnow on the border between Gwent and Herefordshire. Follow the course of each river in turn and you will not be disappointed for they flow through a land of history and great beauty. On the Welsh side of Offa's Dyke the Honddu runs through a mountain fastness where saints and noble lords sought peace and sanctuary. The Monnow and the Dore run through a fertile land where ancient stones, chambered barrows, castles and churches are tangible milestones of the past. All these river valleys can be entered from the border town of Hay-on-Wye.

The Honddu Valley

From Hay a lane climbs alongside the Dulas Brook up to one of the coldest and most exposed passes in Wales. This narrow wind-swept *bwlch*, between Hay Bluff and the Twmpa, is known as Bwlch-yr-Efengel, 'The Pass of the Evangelist', but generally called 'Gospel Pass'. St Peter and his brother apostle Paul are said to have come this way to bring the message of Christianity to the pagan tribes of Wales. After leaving the gap the valley soon narrows, the steep mountains thrusting probing spurs to dictate the direction of road and river. A few miles away at Capel-y-ffin the border is crossed from Breconshire (Powys) into Gwent. During the 1860s Father Ignatius, (Joseph Lycecester Lyne) an Anglican monk, came here to build a monastery and revive the Benedictine order. He caused some confusion by giving it the same

The wild and windswept pass through the Black Mountains known as Bwlch-yr-Efengel, 'the Pass of the Evangelist'.

Capel y Ffin, a few miles from Gospel Pass, has a quaint little church with a timber bell-turret.

name by which an ancient priory about four miles further down the valley was called. Through lack of funds his project failed so now there is little left to see, but the small hamlet has its church, a simple little building with a square slatted timber belfry, described by the Reverend Francis Kilvert as 'an old chapel, short, stout and boxy, with its little bell-turret – the whole building reminding me of an owl'.

From Capel-y-ffin the narrow twisting road runs down the valley to the picturesque ruins of Llanthony Priory – Llanddewi Nant Honddu, 'The Church of St David in the Valley of the Honddu'. The first church which stood here, built of mud and wattle, was a hermitage-chapel for St David in the 6th century. He lived there for many years, subsisting, so it is said, on the wild leeks which grew along the banks of the Honddu, so it is possible to believe that this was the reason for Wales selecting the leek as a national emblem. The fine priory which rose from the site of St David's lowly Christian cell was built by William de Lacy, a Norman soldier, and Ernisus, chaplain to King Henry I and Queen Maud. William and Ernisus decided to dwell in this hallowed spot for the rest of their lives. About 700 years later Gerald, the Welsh historian wrote,

> In the deep Vale of Ewyas which is about an arrow-shot broad, encircled on all sites by lofty mountains stands the church of St John the Baptist . . . it was founded by two hermits, in honour of the retired life, far removed from the bustle of mankind, in a solitary vale watered by the river Hodeni.
>
> Here the monks, sitting in their cloisters, enjoying the fresh air, when they happen to look up to the horizon, behold the tops of the mountains, as it were, touching the heavens, and the herds of wild deer feeding on their summits.

Before his sudden conversion William de Lacy had led a joyous life and, as a soldier of the Earl of Hereford he would have shared in the plunder and pillage of this part of the Welsh Marches. For these reasons his conversion was dramatic, for he now welcomed a life of discomfort and austerity, wearing over his armour a hair shirt, and although the armour became worn out with rust and age he wore it for the rest of his life. He gladly forsook the comfort and riches which he had previously enjoyed to dwell poor in the house of God. Through the ravages of war and local strife between the Welsh who often disturbed the peace of the inmates of the priory it was, according to an account written by one of its monks, 'reduced to such straits that the monks had no breeches, and could not, with decency, attend Divine Services'.

From Llanthony the valley road runs close to the Honddu to Cwmyoy, a small hamlet uncomfortably close to an almost vertical cliff. Some years ago a landslide caused part of the cliff to fall, threatening to

Llanthony Priory, according to tradition, was founded on the site where St. David built a lowly mud and wattle hermitage.

push the small church and houses into the river. As a result of this near-disaster the tower and walls of the church lean away at different angles, and some years ago further subsidence made it necessary to close the village school. The origin of St Martin's church is ancient, for it is supposed that one was built here before the Norman Conquest. The finding of a medieval cross suggests that pilgrims coming through the valley on their way to St David's shrine sought rest and shelter at the little church.

The end of the valley is reached where two mountain spurs are topped with prehistoric earthworks which overlook the flat plainlands of Gwent and Herefordshire. Here the Honddu, and a minor stream, join the Monnow to form a moat which almost encircles the historic manor of Allterynys. This ancient house was once the home of the famous Cecil family whose forefathers, the Sytsyllts, were almost wiped out by the infamous Marcher Lord, William de Braose, who trapped them at Abergavenny Castle. William Cecil was a powerful supporter of Queen Elizabeth I, and one who helped her relinquish the firm grip of the Catholic Church.

The Monnow Valley

The head of the Monnow Valley is reached by taking the same road from Hay-on-Wye to Gospel Pass. At the top of Cusop Dingle a junction is reached which crosses the Welsh border just north of Offa's Dyke into Herefordshire. Nearby are the scant remains of Craswall Priory, for most of its stones were taken and used by the local people to build the walls of barns and other farm buildings. On a bend, just before the narrow mountain road crosses the Monnow, stands a picturesque little border church with a close-boarded wooden turret astride a medieval roof. Against one of the external walls are traces of a games-court, so perhaps the game of Fives *did* originate in this mountain valley and not at Eton College? The flat area against the church wall and the wooden shutters to protect the glass in the windows give credence to the assertion that ball-games were once played there. The stone bench-seats recessed into the external walls may have been used by spectators.

Just before reaching Longtown, the valley's largest village, you can cross the Olchon Brook at Pen-pwll-sond and make a short tour of the small but picturesque Olchon Valley. The road soon turns back northwards, running in the deep shadows cast by the cliffs of Black and Red Daren. At the end of the road is a spot marked on the map as Blaen Olchon where a track leads to the summit of Black Hill, then onwards to the ridge of Hay Bluff. The walk along the track is pleasant and easy, well worth taking for the splendid view it offers over the plains of

View of the beautiful Llanthony Valley towards Gospel Pass.

The tower and walls of Cwmyoy church lean away at precarious angles.

south-west Herefordshire between the Black Mountains and the Wye.

Many of the early castles which the Norman Marcher Lords raised between the eastern flank of the Black Mountains and the Wye were simple, but well planned, motte and bailey earthworks, but at Longtown they soon raised above their earthwork defences a strong stone keep surrounded by a series of outer wards extending over an area of three acres. The massive keep, with ten feet thick walls, was strong enough to resist the most determined attack from their foes who came over Offa's Dyke. Squeezed between the Olchon Brook and the Monnow the village, long and straggling, is suitably named. Some interesting old houses line the main street; one, at the north end of the village, is Court House which dates from the closing years of the 17th century. It is supposed to stand on the site of a building used for trials in the days when the castle was occupied; this would account for its name, and also by the fact that the present building was also used as a Court of Justice until it became an inn. It is now an Adventure Centre administered by the Education Department of the County Borough of Northampton. The Centre provides excellent facilities for all facets of youth adventure training, and is also well equipped for pony-trekking, canoeing, rock climbing and safe exploration of the surrounding countryside.

South of Longtown is Clodock where the church is dedicated to St Clydawg, grandson of King Brychan of Breconshire. Clydawg was known for his good deeds, and after he was murdered by a jealous rival he was revered as a saint. On the day of his burial the oxen pulling his funeral cart refused to cross a tributary of the Monnow, so he was buried nearby. The enclosure, or *llan*, which surrounded his grave became known as Llan-y-Merthyr Clydawg, 'The Enclosure of Martyr Clydawg'. Churches built on this site date from 400 AD to 1066 AD, and when some alterations were in progress about 1918 a memorial stone was discovered of pre-Conquest period. The inscription on it was found difficult to read, but an acceptable translation is that,

This tomb has the remains of that
faithful woman, the dear wife of
Guinnda who herself was resident
in this place.

When Walterstone is reached road and river pass over the border back into Gwent. It is worth climbing the hill past the church up to an ancient fort for excellent views of the countryside and mountains. Skirrid Fawr, 'The Holy Mountain', like a miniature Alpine peak, and the Sugar Loaf mountain above Abergavenny present an attractive picture, then above Oldcastle, the next place we shall visit, rises the almost vertical eastern wall of the Black Mountains. Oldcastle at the end of a lane is a small hamlet known only for the fact that it bears the same name as Sir John Oldcastle, the Lollard martyr, who was a close friend of Prince Hal of Monmouth before he became King Henry V. After crossing the river the road through the Monnow Valley ends at Pandy, a small village on the A465 Abergavenny to Hereford trunk road.

The Valley of the Dore

To the Welsh this was the Dwr Valley, for as *dwr* was their word for water they considered it more appropriate than the one given to the valley by the Normans which means golden. The Norman name has survived for all maps of this area show it as the 'Golden Valley'.

Merbach Hill, the birthplace of the Dore river, marks the northern entrance to this valley which is an Arcadian land of meadowland and cornfield. Centuries ago this fertile land belonged to the Welsh, an ownership which proved unfortunate for a band of Highlanders in flight after the Battle of Worcester. They thought little harm could come to them in such a peaceful spot, so decided to rest awhile on the bank of the river, but before they had time to bathe their blistered feet they were ambushed and massacred by the Welsh. This spot, where the Dore 'ran red with blood for three days', is marked on the map as Scotland Bank. From this place of bloody memory a lane climbs up to the ridge of Merbach Hill. On the ridge stands a cromlech known as 'Arthur's Stone', but this might be a corruption of Thor Stone from which Dorstone, the next village along the valley derives its name.

Dorstone, with farms and cottages set amid apple orchards and overlooked by the tower of a Norman church is a peaceful place. Refuge was sought here by one of the baron-knights who hastened to rid their king of 'that turbulent priest', Archbishop Thomas a Becket, whom they murdered on the altar steps of Canterbury Cathedral in 1117. The penitent Thomas de Britto sought sanctuary and forgiveness here by spending the rest of his life in the service of God. When the church was restored some years ago his tomb was discovered, and in it a pewter chalice which can now be seen in a glass-fronted recess of the chancel wall.

Lanes climb hills and run through *cwms* from both sides of the valley road to prehistoric camps, castles, churches and other places of historic interest. From Merbach ridge a road drops down to Bredwardine where the Wye flows past the site of a motte and bailey fort which was hurriedly constructed by a Marcher Lord to protect his land and booty from the Welsh who sought to control and hold as many river crossings as they could. The church at Bredwardine, built soon after the Conquest, has several interesting features; one is a doorway with a carved

80

lintel decorated with unidentifiable monsters. Inside are two effigies, one, of stone, is badly mutilated, but the other, executed in alabaster, is in almost perfect condition. On it lies the armour-clad figure of Sir Roger Vaughan who shared with David Gam of Gwent the honour of saving their king's life at Agincourt. David Gam is credited as being the Ffluellen of Shakespeare's Henry V. Near to Bredwardine are picturesque cottages and farmhouses; one of the finest is hidden among trees on the fringe of Moccas Park. This is Bodcot Farm, a stone and half-timbered house in a beautiful setting alongside a disused lane – a lane which may once have been the main route over Merbach Hill to Dorstone.

There are other interesting places to explore along both banks of the Wye, but on this journey it is better to return to Dorstone and complete our exploration of the Golden Valley. Just outside Dorstone is Snodhill Court near the ruins of a castle which Queen Elizabeth I is supposed to have made a 'handsome' present of to the Earl of Leicester. By all accounts he did not care to live there for he soon disposed of it. There is little to see of the old castle, possibly because it was dismantled to provide building material for the nearby Court, a place, if the stories are true, of ghostly funeral processions and haunted rooms.

Two roads lead to Peterchurch, one along the west bank of the river, or, from Dorstone, the B4348 on the other side of the river. When St Peter reached the *bwlch* above Hay-on-Wye, having tired of overgrown valleys and windswept mountain passes, he left St Paul to seek more sheltered pastures. He found the place he was looking for after following a stream from Urishay Common down to the Golden Valley and the Dore river. After founding a church and the settlement which grew around it he called it Peterchurch. To preserve the memory of his visit he sanctified the waters of a well for baptism of his converts. On the wall of the church is an effigy of a great fish with a golden chain about its neck; it is supposed to have been caught in the Dore, collar and all. Another legend insists that the piscatorial monster was caught by St Peter who, after attaching a gold chain to it, dropped it in the well. Whichever story is true, the valuable necklet has disappeared. Anyway the plaster effigy of the huge fish would be more suitable on the wall of a riverside pub than in a church.

On a hill above Peterchurch is Urishay, a strange atmospheric place, where the ruins of a large mansion overlook the mounds of an early fortress. The house was built in the 16th century by Urry of Hay (Hay means an enclosure) and from him the place derives its name. The sight of the cracked walls and broken mullions of the windows is depressing, conveying a feeling that one is looking at a three dimensional illustration from Poe's *Fall of the House of Usher*. Adjacent to the earthworks stands a ruined chapel of uncertain date. Like the ruined mansion it is in a

Bodcot Farm is typical of the 'magpie' black and white timber buildings of Herefordshire.

deplorable state and at some time, a visitor with a sense of history and occasion, was prompted to scrawl *ICHABOD* on the chancel wall; an appropriate graffito for the glory has indeed departed!

Two miles away are the villages of Vowchurch and Turnastone, each having their own church. Vowchurch was the home of the elder of two sisters who decided to finance the building of a church. For some reason they quarrelled and commenced building separate churches – the elder sister exclaiming that 'I *vow* to build my church before you *turn a stone* of yours'. So the villages were named Vowchurch and Turnastone. Both are beautifully situated; Vowchurch on the river bank, and Turnastone set among ancient yews.

Further down the valley a road crosses the river where a narrow lane leaves it to Bacton Church built on a knoll below the Black Mountains. Inside the parish church is an interesting memorial to Blanche Parry, a lady associated with the virgin queen in fiction and history. The Tudor memorial shows Blanche kneeling in front of Queen Elizabeth I pledging that she, too, will remain a virgin all her life, and the lines on the tomb confirm her pledge. They say,

A maede in Court and never no man's wife,
Swore of Queen Elizabeth's *bedd* chamber allwaye,
Wythe maeden Queen, a maede dyd ende my lyffe.

It is interesting to note the spelling, with the double 'd' of the word bed, for it is spelt the same way in Welsh.

About two miles away is the monastic building of Abbey Dore near the outlet of the Golden Valley. Robert, Earl of Ewyas Harold, founded the abbey here in about 1150. The name for it must have been established, for the Norman-French word for gold is *D'ore*. The Marcher barons were realists, so there can be little doubt that Robert made sure that the labour of the Cistercian monks of the abbey would supply him with material benefit in his lifetime, and that their prayers would go a long way to ensure his spiritual well-being in afterlife. After the Dissolution in 1634 much of the beautiful building was destroyed, and stones, lead and timber taken for use in building nearby houses and farms. However, enough remained to encourage Lord Scudamore of Kentchurch Court to carry out work of partial restoration. In later years the interior was enriched with an elaborately carved chancel screen, designed and constructed by John Abel, the royally appointed carpenter of King Charles I.

At Ewyas Harold is a mound above the Dulas Brook marking the site of a castle battered by Saxon, Welsh and Norman. Its early history is obscure, and the historian Leland's account is somewhat uncertain. He wrote,

Abbey Dore, the Cistercian abbey built in the Golden Valley in 1150, taking its name from the Norman-French 'dore', the word for gold.

The fame goeth that Kynge Harold had a son named Harold, and of this Harold part of Ewis was named Ewis Harold. The fame is that the castell of Map-Harold was buildid of Harold, afore he was Kynge, and when he overcame the Walsche-men, Harold gave the castell to his bastard.

When the Norman masons completed the stone castle of Ewyas Harold it is feasible to assume they were sent to build a church at Rowlstone, one which contains some of the richest stone carvings in Herefordshire. The tympanum over the south doorway and the chancel arch are masterpieces of Celtic-Norman work. The church is dedicated to St Peter, and inside are features which confirm this. In the sanctuary are metal candle brackets decorated with cocks, and to remind one of how St Peter was crucified upside-down the capitals of the chancel arch are faced with a carving of him head downwards.

One mile from Ewyas Harold the main road (A465) to Hereford is reached at Pontrilas where the Dulas and Worm streams join the River Dore. Further north is St Devereux, a French name but one probably derived from that of St Dyfrig, but this is of less importance than that half a mile away at Kilpeck is a mound which once supported a famous Marcher stronghold. The castle has all but disappeared, but below the mound is one of the finest specimens of a Norman church in the whole of Britain, and is the Mecca of architect and historian.

The church stands where the Saxons built one about the year 650. Kilpeck is derived from an ancient British word Kil, or Cell, linked with Pedic it was known as the Cell of Pedric. William FitzNorman raised his castle on the mound, but being occupied in protecting his illgotten gains from the Celts it was left to his grandson Hugh to build the church. Since completion, about the middle of the 12th century, there has been little alteration. Official records affirm that the castle, church and village combine to make Kilpeck 'One of the most important rural medieval sites in England'. It certainly has the most famous Norman entrance doorway in Britain, its columned jambs richly carved and decorated with Biblical scenes. Mixed with them are figures of warriors wearing pointed caps, ribbed jerkins and trews held up by knotted scarfs. The arched tympanum has a conventional vine-spray pattern enclosed by recessed arches embellished with carvings of mythical birds and beasties. Around the eaves projecting stone corbels carved with strange designs, and some with leering faces, overlook the churchyard. Judging from the inventiveness of design and execution it is evident that these early craftsmen suffered little from the torments of repression. Or did they? The work of these skilled stone-carvers has already been seen at churches in Eardisley (page 62) and at Rowlstone, which has already been described in this chapter.

A Saxon church existed at Kilpeck in AD 650. On the same site the Normans built a church which must have the finest entrance in all of Britain.

The next area to be explored, west of Offa's Dyke, is the narrow strip of land between the B4352 road and the Wye where the river flows through the lowlands from Bredwardine to the city of Hereford. The B4352 runs westwards from the Hereford road, its junction indicated by a signpost pointing the way to Clehonger and Madley. Keeping close company with the Wye the road takes you through meadowlands and ploughed fields of a rich-red colour irrigated by many nameless streams. After crossing a brook a signpost on the right directs the way to Eaton Bishop where you will find a magnificent church with windows filled with glass dating back to the last years of the 12th century, and having symbolic designs in company with the figures of saints and holy men. At Madley, just a short distance away, the size of the church here suggests that Madley must once have been a very important place, particularly if the north porch had been the transept of an earlier church. With a large nave and two side aisles the church has the dimensions of a lesser cathedral, and it also has a crypt. Like Fairford, in the Cotswolds, the church is famous for its stained glass. The Fairford windows frightened the medieval congregation with goblin figures, and they show, in vivid detail, the tortures they could look forward to if sent to Hades. The Madley windows have gentler themes, for the 15th century glaziers arranged the segments of coloured glass to show the Presentation at the Temple, the Adoration of the Magi, the women at the Holy Sepulchre, and the Last Supper.

Throughout Wales a number of places claim to be the last resting place of Owain Glyndwr. All of the claims are plausible, but it is more likely that the old warrior, harried and weary, came to spend the last days of his life with his daughter at Monnington Court on the north bank of the Wye. The Court and church stand side by side, conveniently so if it is true that the Welsh leader came here to die, and was carried to rest in a churchyard grave. He came from a kingly stock, so it is sad to be told that this brave man, 'not in the roll of common men', lies in an unmarked grave.

Our interesting journey through this beautiful and historic part of the Celtic borderland between the Welsh mountains and the Wye ends at Bredwardine.

The Castles of the Monnow

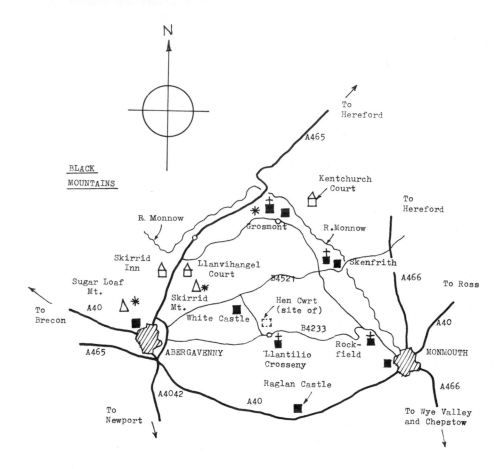

CHAPTER SIX

The Castles of the Monnow

In the previous chapter a journey along the banks of the Monnow ended at the small village of Pandy on the main Abergavenny to Hereford trunk road. From here the river turns northwards to flow through the lowland pastures of Gwent to join with the Wye at Monmouth town. This corner of Gwent is steeped in history and played an important part in the story of this Celtic borderland. Proof of this can be found in many places along the banks of the Monnow.

South of Pandy is Llanfihangel Crucorney, known for having an ancient inn which claims to be the oldest in Wales, having first opened its doors just half a century after the Norman invasion, and was then known as Millbrook. Between 1100 and 1500 offenders were brought there for trial, and it is recorded that in the early years of the 12th century John and James Crowther were tried and sentenced there. James for robbery, and John, who was hanged from a beam above the staircase, for sheep stealing. It is believed that the notorious Judge Jeffreys presided over a Court held during the 17th century to deal with those who took part in a local Papist plot which took place in Gwent about 1679. Dispensation of justice in the courtroom of the Skirrid Inn probably gave him a taste for power over life and death when he dealt with the king's enemies at the Bloody Assize in 1685. Halfway up the staircase you can see a small room (now used as a bathroom) where those sentenced to death spent their last miserable night before being hanged from the beam above the staircase well. Scorch marks caused by the drag of the hangman's rope can still be seen, so there is little wonder that the ghosts of those hanged here are said to haunt the old inn.

In parkland opposite the inn is Llanfihangel Court, a Tudor mansion replacing an earlier house which stood on the same site in the reign of King Henry VI. It is probably the most picturesque manor house in Gwent, with a magnificent approach by way of a long flight of stone steps rising up between grass terraces. Queen Elizabeth I is said to have been entertained here, and the ceiling of the bedroom she used is decorated with an artistic pattern of Tudor roses and Fleur-de-lis. It is also claimed that King Charles I slept here, and an oak panel over one of the fireplaces was once the head of the bed in which he slept. On it is carved a Welsh motto, 'Kofia dy Ddechre', which means 'Remember thy

The Skirrid Inn is the oldest in Wales. It served as a Court and a place of execution. Reputed to be haunted by those who were hanged from a beam above the staircase well.

Skirrid Fawr, 'the Holy Mountain'. Many legends are attached to this mountain, and there are scant remains of a chapel on the summit.

Origin'. As a memento of his visit the king left a wooden panel with his arms painted on it and inlaid with mother-of-pearl. It would be strange if such an old house did not have a secret hiding place and, of course, a resident ghost; in fact it has both. The ghost is known as 'The White Lady of Llanfihangel Court'. At midnight she walks through the hall, and after descending the terrace steps, disappears into a wood which is called 'Lady Wood'. Her visitations are punctual, for if it is Summer the clock strikes *one* when she appears. Years ago a skeleton with a bullet hole through the skull was found buried beneath the lawn in front of the house.

Just beyond the Skirrid Inn a signpost points the way to Grosmont by way of Campston Hill. Rising from the fields along the south side of the hill is the north flank of the alpine-shaped Skirrid Fawr, 'The Holy Mountain', famous in legend and shrouded in superstition. Was the great chasm in its western flank really caused when the mountain was shattered by lightning during the storm following the Crucifixion; was the fissure made by the sharp prow of Noah's Ark as it sailed over the summit – or was it caused by a landslide brought about by a geological fault? On the summit, 1,600 feet above sea level, a few stones and depressions in the ground indicate the site of St Michael's chapel where, in 1680, the Papist's gathered for Mass. Some insist that the depressions were made by the heels of Jack o' Kent when he leaped across the valley to the top of the Sugar Loaf mountain. It was once thought that the soil around the site of the chapel was holy, and the local country-folk gathered it to spread on the floors of their cattle sheds to ward off disease. These are but a few strange stories connected with this hill overlooking the fields of Gwent and Herefordshire.

Proof of the part this land played in shaping history is found along the banks of the Monnow river, a stream which irrigates the lush pasture lands of north-east Gwent. The castles of Grosmont and Skenfrith stand close to the Monnow and, with nearby Whitecastle they were built by the Normans as a carefully planned group of fortifications to hold down the Welsh. Churchyard considered the 'Three Castles' as an important defensive unit when he wrote,

> Three castles fayre are in goodly ground,
> Grosmont is one, on hill it buildid was;
> Skenfrith the next, in valley it was found,
> Whitecastle is the third, of worthie fame,
> The country round doth bear Whit Castle's name;
> A Statlie seat, a lofty princlie place,
> Whose beauty gives simple soyle some grace.

At the top of Campston Hill a splendid viewpoint is reached. To the

Grosmont Castle, built on a mound captured from the Welsh. The wild roses growing around this Lancastrian stronghold gave it the title of 'the Castle of the Red Rose.'

west, receding in the hazy distance, are the repetitive shapes of the out-thrust spurs of the Black Mountains. Below the mountains the Monnow, its course punctuated by sunlight and translucent shadow, flows northwards to the Herefordshire border, then eastwards to Kentchurch where it curves away in a great loop round Cupid's Hill to Grosmont and the hills of Gwent. Grosmont, on a hill above the Monnow, was once an important and thriving town with royal and Lancastrian connections, but when the power of the Red Rose declined so did the town. Before then it had been a place of consequence, having a charter and the right to have a mayor and an official ale-taster. There is little left today to indicate that it was once a busy and prosperous town.

On top of Grosmont hill the Welsh dug a deep ditch, and on the mounded excavation they built a protective palisade. When the Normans drove the Welsh away they replaced their primitive fortress with a more durable one built of stone. Upon every side, except that facing the village, the hillside drops steeply down to the Monnow which served as a natural outer moat. This eyric of the Lords Marchers must have been a fine castle, for here and there are features which show that it had been a place of comfort for kings and barons. To obtain immediate security and comfort the Normans first built a strong keep, than afterwards a large hall which had a solar at ground level with the windows placed to benefit from the morning and late evening sun. When the weather was cold they warmed themselves in front of large fireplaces which had elegant chimneys. After ensuring their safety from Welsh attack they spent the following twenty years or so in building an outer ward with three strong towers. Inside can still be seen traces of dressed stonework framing the openings of doors and windows.

In 1233 King Henry III and his wife Eleanor were entertaining many of their foreign favourites at the castle. News of this, and that their king was about to hand over large portions of their estates to the foreigners, angered the Lords Marchers. Supported by Welsh partisans, who were always ready to help oust a Norman from his castle, they joined in an attack which caused discomfort, and not a little embarrassment to the king and his queen when they saw their guests forced to scramble across the castle ditch in their night attire. Accounts of this incident vary, but it seems that the Marcher Lords and their Welsh allies were more concerned in the capture of loot than clearing the castle of the foreign adventurers.

Wild red roses grew in the castle gardens, so it became known as 'The Castle of the Red Rose', a flower which became a Lancastrian emblem. As the Yorkists displayed the sign of the 'White Rose', this was a sensible decision. After defeating their foes the Yorkists left the castle in poor condition, but enough of it was left standing to house the forces who defended it in 1405 against an army sent by Owain Glyndwr.

Skenfrith Castle, built by the Normans to form a trilateral group of fortresses to protect and hold their grip of the north-east corner of Gwent.

Despite a fierce Welsh attack the Anglo-Norman garrison held out until Prince Hal of Monmouth, then a boy of about eighteen or nineteen, came with reinforcements from Hereford. The trained troops swept the Welsh away in disorder, slaying 800 of them. Encouraged by his victory the young prince marched his army to Brecon where they fought and defeated the Welsh again, and captured Glyndwr's son. In a message to his father the prince said that he would have sent his important captive as well – 'but he cannot yet ride with ease'.

Near the castle the Normans built a church, a larger than normal building whose different architectural styles suggest that constructional progress was slow, probably due to constant interruption from the Welsh. Inside is a large mutilated stone effigy said to be of Henry of Lancaster. Grosmont has memories of John of Kent who had such magical powers that Satan had to intervene. John made a pact with him that he should have his body after death, but knowing that Satan would not go near a holy place he arranged for his body to be buried under the walls of this sanctified building. Who John was is uncertain; some say that he was Owain Glyndwr, others that he was John of Gaunt, but it is more likely that he was a parish priest of nearby Kentchurch.

Kentchurch Court, a fortified manor house, dates from the 14th century, and was the home of the Scudamores. Several members of this family, fighting for the Lancastrian cause, died at Mortimer's Cross in 1461. This house is another which claims to have sheltered Glyndwr during the last years of his life; this is feasible, for one of his three daughters married Sir John Scudamore who owned the manor then. In 1824 the historic house was repaired and improved by John Nash, the famous London architect who designed Buckingham Palace.

Skenfrith is the second Monnow-side castle of the trilateral group of Norman fortifications built to guard the borderland of north-east Gwent. With a castle, a mill and a pretty timber-belfried church the village of Skenfrith is charming. It takes its name from Ynys Cynfraeth, which suggests an island where Cynfraeth, a 6th century chieftain, built his fort. On this site the present castle stands, the battered walls of the ward enclosure dominating the village and encircling the keep built on a small island above the surrounding land and river.

There is a legend telling of treasure buried within the curtain walls, and there is a document in the British Museum which gives the story credence. It was written by a Welshman in the hope that it would persuade the Crown to release him from his dungeon prison in the Tower of London. The document, sent to the royal treasurer, is dated 28th April 1589. In a quaint style it reads,

The voyce of the country goeth there is a dyvill and his dame, one sits upon a hogshead of gold, the other upon a hogshead of silver.

Whitecastle, closely linked with the Norman fortresses of Skenfrith and Grosmont, was the most powerful of the border strongholds.

The hogsheads in the face of their custodians, *Taffy* engages to unearth from beneath the courtyard, without any charge to the Quene or your lordships. If the treasure be there I will look for something from your lordships, for the country saith there is great treasure.

It must all have sounded very plausible, and the writer very aware of the queen's interest in enrichment of the royal coffers. It is also interesting to note that even in Elizabethan times a Welshman expected to be known as a *Taffy*.

Skenfrith church, its square squat tower topped with a wooden dovecote roof, is the prettiest in Gwent. Inside are features and relics of the past. John Morgan, the last custodian of the castle and his wife lie beneath a large altar-tomb. It is dated 1557, and on the top are the incised figures of John and Anne; on the sides are their 'weepers', their four sons and four daughters – all dressed in elaborate clothes of the period. Near their tomb is the large box-like family pew which enabled them to sit away from the common people, and in comparative comfort. A glass-fronted case on the wall encloses a cope worked in coloured silks, an ecclesiastical garment said to have been a gift from King John, although another legend claims that it was given to the church by Queen Eleanor who embroidered it during a stay at the castle when her husband, Henry III, was campaigning against the Welsh.

Garway, on the English side of the Monnow, also has an interesting church; it is dedicated to St Michael and is one of six Knights Templar churches in England. The order was originated by a small band of French knights in 1131 who protected pilgrims on their way to the Holy Sepulchre. Growing rich and powerful the members of the Order did not always live up to their high ideals, so it is possible that the detached tower of Garway church became a place of refuge from the hostility of their embittered parishioners. A window corbel is carved with the head of a Grand Master of their Order, and here and there are symbolic carvings which would be understood by present day Masonic brethren. To ensure a plentiful supply of fresh meat, brother Richard, in 1326, built a splendid columbarium; it is about 18 feet in diameter with walls 4 feet thick. An aperture at the top of the circular building provided access for the pigeons who had as many as 666 nesting holes to chose from.

Skenfrith was an outpost, and Grosmont provided comfortable quarters for visiting barons and their servants, but Whitecastle was a true warriors stronghold, and the most exposed of the three castles. Although it does not stand on the banks of the Monnow it must be considered in context with the other two. Whitecastle stands on a hill about five or six miles from the other two, and as an arrowhead thrusting into Welsh territory it would be the first to be attacked. The

The Monnow Bridge and Gateway, the only one of its kind in Britain. Built by the Normans to defend the river crossing to Monmouth town.

Normans realised this when they took and developed the first primitive fortress built by Gwyn-ap-Gwaethfod before the Norman Conquest. Some sort of defences stood here in the middle of the 11th century, owned by Gwyn, a son of a prince of Cardigan. Gwyn is the Welsh word for white, so it is likely that it was known as Gwyn's Castle, and it is believed that the stonework was covered with a coating of white plaster. Gwyn, old and blind, lost his castle to one of the early Norman invaders. He appealed to the Red King (Rufus) saying, 'Give me a chance to fight the new lord on equal terms and I will prove that I am the better man'. His suggestion appealed to the Norman king for he arranged that Gwyn should meet his opponent in a darkened room, with no quarter asked for or given. From this trial by combat the Welshman emerged victorious and won his castle back.

The visitor will soon be convinced that nothing had been spared in time or labour to ensure that Whitecastle would be one of the most powerful of the border strongholds, and that the deep water-filled moat made the taking of the castle a very difficult task. Being so closely linked with Grosmont and Skenfrith its history is similar, and after the Wars of the Roses the Yorkists saw that Whitecastle also became untenable. On top of one of the north gateway towers a wooden platform provides a safe vantage point, and from it the visitor can see that the large outer ward is surrounded on three sides by another moat. It will also be appreciated why the Normans took and improved the ancient fortress of Gwyn-ap-Gwaethfod on this isolated hill in the centre of a mountain-rimmed basin.

From the castle a lane runs southwards to the village of Llantilio Crosseny on the B4233 road which will take you to Monmouth and the most illustrious of the Monnow castles. At the junction of the lane with the Monmouth road is a moated island site on which stood Hen Cwrt, (Old Court) the home of Sir David Gam who won immortal fame when he helped to save the life of his king at Agincourt. Sir David was a brave man, and when King Henry V asked for his estimation of the size of the French army, he replied, 'enough to be killed, enough to be taken prisoner, and enough to run away'.

Llantilio Crosseny derives its name partly from the church, for Llantilio means 'the church of Teilo', and partly from Ynyr, the name of a Welsh king of this part of Gwent; and Crosseny means 'the Cross of Ynyr'. In the 6th century St Teilo was Bishop of Llandaff, and his powerful prayers are said to have brought victory to the Welsh when they fought the Saxons near here in AD 596. The present church dates from the 13th century, but the mound on which it stands is the hallowed ground where St Teilo knelt to pray for the victory of his Welsh kinsmen.

Soon after reaching a severe hairpin bend near Rockfield the road

Castle House, elegant and well proportioned, dates from 1673. The interior has several interesting features and fine plaster ceilings.

follows the Monnow to the county town of Monmouth, and after crossing the river over the ancient bridge with its Norman gatehouse you will soon arrive in the centre of the town at Agincourt Square. From there a short lane leads to another square in front of a ruined castle. Except for the remains of a 12th century tower there is little to see, for the Civil War and subsequent neglect has reduced it to its present state. On the 9th August 1387 King Henry V was born here, and if records are true, in a room which was 58 feet long by 24 feet wide, with walls 10 feet thick. If the rest of the castle matched these proportions it must have been an impressive royal residence.

Also facing the square is a fine house built of large blocks of red sandstone. Known as Castle House it was built in 1673 by the third Marquis of Worcester for his daughter-in-law who wished for her first child to be born and cradled in a house as near as possible to the birthplace of King Henry V.

From Monmouth to Raglan and Abergavenny

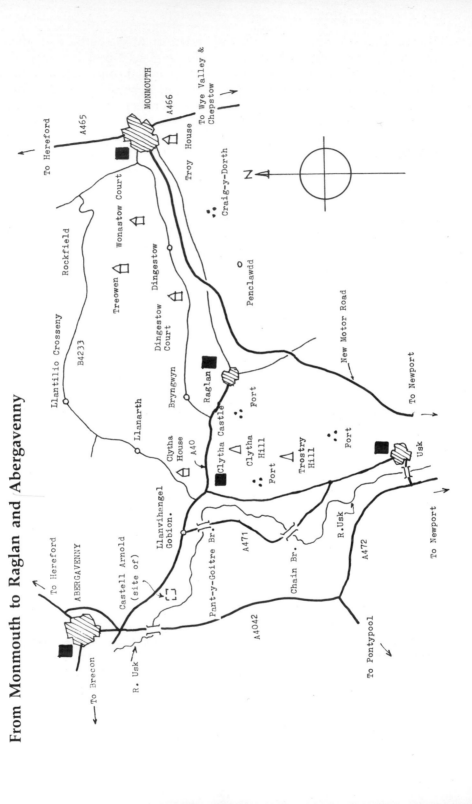

CHAPTER SEVEN

From Monmouth to Raglan and Abergavenny

Several of the first chapters of this book have, for the most part, been about exploring an area of south-east Wales, and the lands between the rivers Wye and Severn, and generally on the English side of Offa's Dyke. Now from Monmouth, which straddles the dyke at a point where it changes direction to run westwards through the lowlands of Gwent, we continue our explorations on the Welsh side of old Offa's boundary.

South of Monmouth a short lane leads from the old A40 trunk road (now subsidiary to a new motor road) to the entrance gates of Troy House, one of the most historic houses in Gwent. Associated with kings and many noble families Troy House has played a prominent part in the history of our land. It is reputed to have been designed by Inigo Jones, but old records assert that it existed before the famous architect was born. The exterior, although well proportioned, is somewhat dull, but the interior has features which are far more interesting. One of the main rooms with panelled walls and a richly carved fireplace surround, said to have been brought from Raglan Castle, is very beautiful. The plaster ceilings of this, and some other rooms, are well designed, and from the main hall an impressive staircase rises to the upper floors.

The house, once the home of the Dukes of Beaufort, has been used as a convent, and when the house was used for this purpose a modern, but tastefully designed, chapel was added. Within recent years it was used by the Catholic Church and the Gwent County Council as a home for delinquent girls. In its time the house has contained many treasures. About 1850 it was reported that in the hall stood the battle-armour that King Henry V, who was born at Monmouth Castle, wore at Agincourt, and in one of the bedrooms was a cradle, brought from the castle, in which he slept as a baby. There is no reliable information as to where these interesting relics now are, or if they were genuine.

Not far south-west of Troy House is a conical tree-clad hill known as Craig-y-dorth which is also connected with the victor of Agincourt, and also with his fiercest enemy Owain Glyndwr. It was from this hill, after the Battle of Shrewsbury in 1403, that Glyndwr beat off an English army sent to destroy him. The Welsh forces, led by Glyndwr, were more than a match for the English, and chased them back to the Monnow gateway. Owain was elated at his victory, and when Shakespeare was writing his

Troy House near Monmouth, associated with kings and nobles it played a prominent part in the history of the Marches of Wales.

Treowen Mansion, the home of the Herberts, a family also associated with the turbulent history of Wales and the Marches.

Henry IV, Part I, he must have remembered the battle fought on Craig-y-dorth Hill, making Glyndwr exclaim,

'Three times hath Henry Bolingbroke made head
Against my power; thrice from the banks of Wye
And sandy-bottomed Severn, have I sent
Him bootless home; and weather-beaten back'.

From Over Monnow a narrow unclassified road runs alongside the new motor road through several places of interest before it joins the main A40 road to Abergavenny just west of Raglan. About two miles away from Monmouth is Wonastow lying in the shelter of a wooded hill. The small church here is dedicated to St Wonno who, with two other saints, Illtud and Tyfodwg, established a *llan* on a hill in Glamorgan, where the settlement which grew around their sanctuary became known as Llantrisant, 'The Church of the Three Saints'. Wonastow Court, held for King Charles I during the Civil War, stands on a knoll above the river Trothy in company with other houses of age and charm – some of them associated with the names of noble county families.

Between Wonastow and Dingestow the road is marked on the map by the curious name of Jingle Street passing close to Dingestow Court which was built in 1623. Insensitive restoration is evident here, for the falseness of the 'Elizabethan' facade is obvious to all. A mound above the Trothy once supported a castle whose memory is perpetuated in a grim story which is still preserved. The castle, probably a motte and bailey, was initiated by the Marcher Lord, William de Braose, the cruel Lord of Abergavenny. Hearing that he and his compatriot, Ranalf Poer, Sheriff of Hereford, were visiting to supervise the constructional work the Welsh stormed across the Trothy and slew Ranalf and those working on the castle. In the confusion De Braose hid in a ditch, escaping discovery and certain death when an unexpected band of Norman soldiers arrived to chase away the Welsh.

About a mile away is another splendid manor house, one which is also reputed to have been designed by Inigo Jones; although smaller than Troy House it is considerably more beautiful. If the famous architect did design and build the house he raised it on foundations which supported work of earlier years. This mansion, called Treown, has been well described as 'a square brown house, solid as a Norman keep'. It was originally three stories in height but has been lowered to two. Its finest feature is an ornate entrance porch which bears the arms of the Herberts and other noble families associated with the Welsh Marches. The rooms are spacious, and from the hall a wide, richly decorated staircase rises to the upper rooms. If permission can be obtained from the owner it is well worth visiting. After leaving Dinges-

Dingestow Court dates from about 1623, but the 'Elizabethan' facade is a more recent restoration.

tow a turning on the left, just before reaching Tregare, leads to Raglan Castle, now a ruin, but once the largest and finest medieval fortress in the ancient Kingdom of Gwent.

The picturesque ruins stand above the village on rising ground called Twyn-y-Cerious, 'The Cherry Tump'. About the same time that Lord de Clare built a castle at Usk he laid down the foundations at Raglan of an immense hexagonal tower-keep which, because of the yellow glow of its stonework, became known as the Yellow Tower of Gwent. This formidable five storied keep, with ten feet thick walls, resisted all attacks, and even the bombardment of Civil War canons left it isolated and grim above the moat. The Earl of Pembroke, known as Strongbow, probably completed the tower at about the same time as he was building his mighty circular keep at Pembroke. Strongbow, who might just as well have been called 'Richard the Tower Builder', handed the castle and estates of Raglan to Sir Walter de Bloet as a reward for his help in Ireland. In time the castle and estates passed to Sir William ap Thomas, the son-in-law of Sir David Gam, whose brave deeds and knighthood on the battlefield of Agincourt we have already read about.

Sir William's son, a fine soldier and administrator, became custodian of the castle and also, for a short time, of young Henry Tudor, the young man destined to become a King of England. Edward IV found the Welsh custom for a son to take in the name of his father to be confusing, so when he made William an earl in 1468 he insisted that his name must be changed to Herbert. The brave knight lost not only his ancestral name but also his head to the Lancastrians when they disclaimed the right of sanctuary to him in a church porch at Banbury.

The estates, by marriage, next passed to the Somerset family who were now able to add the name of Raglan to their earldoms of Chepstow and Worcester. This happened in 1514, and with such wealth and high position they were able to add size and further beauty to Raglan Castle, so that it was considered second only to Windsor in mangificence. Until the 5th and last Earl of Worcester surrendered the fortress to the forces of Cromwell on the 19th August 1646 life within its walls was dignified and peaceful.

King Charles stayed there several times, always receiving lavish hospitality and entertainment, facts which impoverished his host. The king enjoyed his visits, and must have been displeased when his enemies made it no longer possible for him to travel through this part of Wales. On his last visit it seems that he realised how financial difficulties resulting from his stay worried his host, so he suggested that the Marquis might levy his tenants to pay for the lavish hospitality he and his followers received. His suggestion was not well received, his host replying that 'it was better to live on a crust than live off one's neighbours'. In view of how previous visits of the king and his courtiers

Raglan Castle is the finest and most elegant in the southern Marches of Wales. Although bombarded by Civil War Cannons the picturesque ruins are still impressive.

Pant-y-Goitre Bridge crosses the River Usk near Llanvihangel Gobion, about three miles away from Abergavenny, one of the Gateways of Wales.

had impoverished him, the reply was obviously very pointed and admonishing.

Not long afterwards Cromwell sent Colonel Morgan to demand the surrender of the castle to Parliament. This happened on the 23rd June 1646, then on the 7th August, having 'finished his work in Monmouthshire (Gwent) except this castle', Sir Thomas Fairfax, staying at Cefn Tilla, home of the present Lord Raglan, requested complete surrender. He did not receive a favourable reply, so on the 14th August he commenced a bombardment of the castle. By this time the defenders were running short of provisions, but although the garrison force of 800 men were reduced to half, and a breach was made in an outer wall, the castle was not taken. On the 19th of August 1646 terms of surrender were negotiated, but not until the heroic Marquis had obtained honourable terms of capitulation, terms which allowed all to march out bearing arms, colours flying, and drums and trumpets sounding. Colonel Fairfax honoured the terms of surrender, but as soon as he left to return to his headquarters across the Bristol Channel, the aged Marquis was seized and imprisoned in a cell in London. He died less than four months after leaving Raglan.

Taking advantage of the situation the local people entered the castle. They drained the moat expecting to find hidden treasure, and even emptied the fish-tanks which contained large carp and other fish. Not finding treasure they then stripped the roofs of lead, and timber and stone was carried away to use as building material. When the Duke of Beaufort became aware of this vandalism he prevented its continuation. Now the fabric is administered by the Government, and works of maintenance are carried out when needed.

Those who visit the historic castle today will have little difficulty in conjuring up a picture of the lovely building when all was gracious and beautiful. Walk through the moulded archway with its double portcullis grooves, then into the spacious Fountain Court, so named because it contained a fountain with crystal clear water playing round a marble horse which was the centre-piece. Leave the Court and climb to the top of the Yellow Tower of Gwent, a height from which the expansive plan of the castle can be appreciated. There is also a panoramic view of the countryside, from the fertile spread of the Usk Valley to the distant hills above Abergavenny, and beyond them the Black Mountains and the sharper heights of the Brecon Beacons.

There are even older fortresses than Raglan, many of them in a tract of land south of the A40 road linking Raglan with Abergavenny. From the A40 a lane can be taken to a fine viewpoint and an ancient site on Bryngwyn Hill, and from there a hillfort on Clytha Hill is easily reached. These, and other forts form a chain of observation points overlooking the lower valley of the Usk. This was soon apparent to the Romans for they fought one of their fiercest battles with the Silures to occupy one of them. Today the hill up which the Romans stormed is known as Coed-y-Bwynydd, 'The Wood of Spears', but this translation, except for the word *coed* (which means a wood) is open to question. It is known that the Romans established a long chain of military posts, often making use of British hillforts, through the Usk Valley from their base at Caerleon to Brecon where they built a permanent fortress of stone.

Before the A40 touches the Usk near Llanfihangel Gobion it goes through a short narrow canyon, emerging at a point where you can reach Clytha Castle, or along a drive up to the Classical portico of Clytha House. The castle, built in 1790, on rising ground south of the A40 may be regarded as a local 'Taj Mahal', for it was erected as a monument of affectionate remembrance to a beloved wife. An inscription tells you that,

> This building was erected in the year 1790, by
> William Jones of Clytha House, Esq.,
> Fourth son of John Jones
> of Llanarth Court, Monmouthshire,
> Husband to Elizabeth, the last surviving child
> of Sir William Morgan of Tredegar, K.B.,
> and grand-daughter of the most noble William,
> Second Duke of Devonshire

Rising from old foundations Clytha House was rebuilt in the 18th century, and belonged to the Herbert family. As so often with the names of Welsh families, where sons take in the names of their forefathers, one is easily confused – so for centuries, until 1848, the Herberts were also known as Jones, a name they adopted when the son of John ap Thomas, a Herbert of Treowen, was named William ap John, and in time John, becoming Jones was retained as a surname. It is said that one of the ladies of Clytha used to drive a carriage drawn by a pair of zebras, followed by two Great Danes.

If you take the A471, crossing the Usk over Pant–y–Goitre Bridge, a lane will bring you to the church of St Mary the Virgin at Llanfair Kilgeddin. Inside this sequestered sanctuary you will see an art-form more usually found in Italian churches. The walls of our public build-ings, and even churches are not immune, are often sprayed with offensive sgraffito, spurted from the aero-spray cans of uncaring cretin vandals – so one is certain to be delighted with true sgraffito work on the walls of the church of St Mary. The frescos here have been carried out by the same method used in decorating the walls of the Roman catacombs and churches. They illustrate the theme of the Benedicite, carried out by an English artist, Heywood Summer, in about 1885. There are few other churches in Britain where similar work can be seen. To produce it the plaster on the walls, whilst still wet, is incised with the picture or decorations then coloured and glazed.

In 1950 Llanfair Kilgeddin became known throughout the world as the birth and training place of Foxhunter, the wonder horse owned by Sir Harry Llewellyn. The only gold medal won for Britain at the Helsinki Olympic Games of 1952 was won by Foxhunter. On a high and windy hill above Abergavenny Sir Harry buried his beloved horse, and set in the outcrop rock a memorial tablet recording the show-jumper's international victories.

Most of the churches in the lower Vale of Usk contain something of interest to the historian and tourist. Within easy reach of the A40 is St Cadoc's church where David ap Howell, a 15th century warrior lies buried. His memorial stone, incised with a Christian cross and a battle-axe, suggests that he was a pious man as well as a valiant soldier. Nearby is a site reminding one of the cruelty of the Norman Marcher Lords. A spot on the map between the A40 road and the Usk is marked on the map as being the *'site of Castle Arnold'*. This primitive Welsh fortress stood here in the 12th century, and was the home of Sytsyllt, a descendant of a King of Gwent. His family were all but wiped out when William de Braose, after murdering Sytsyllt at Abergavenny Castle, made the most of his opportunity by also slaying the Welshman's wife and young son. About seven years later the Welsh revenged this bloody slaughter.

Abergavenny is about three miles away, a busy market town almost encircled by hills, its geographical position making it one of the main entrance gateways to Wales. The history of the town is long and bloodstained – from the days when the Romans crossed the Severn and established their fort of Gobannium there, and for centuries after the Norman invasion. The Romans found the people here more intractible and fierce than anywhere else in Britain, and by the time they had fought their way through Gwent the Silures had become more skilled in warfare and their resistance even tougher. The Roman name of Gobannium given to Abergavenny is confirmed by Antoninus in his Itinerary which recorded the distances between Isca Silurum (Caerleon), Magna Castra (Kenchester), Burrium (Usk), and Gobannium itself.

Fortifications to subjugate the people were essential; the Romans built their forts, and in later years the Normans their castles, and there are more of them in South Wales than in other parts of Britain. A mound was raised above the Usk by Hamelin de Balun soon after the Norman Conquest, and by about 1090 it supported a stone keep. By the time this fortress came into the ownership of William de Braose it had been enlarged, and a large hall stood on ground which is now used as a tennis court. If any part of the castle is haunted by memories of Norman

In the Herbert Chapel of St. Mary's Priory Church at Abergavenny is a fine collection of memorial tombs. This is the tomb of Sir William ap Thomas, father of the first Earl of Pembroke.

treachery and murder it must be here – on a spot which evokes memories of a cruel and bloody massacre.

During the Christmas festivities of 1175 William de Braose invited Sytsyllt ap Dafnawld and other Welsh chieftains to a banquet, making it an occasion when they were all to discuss and agree terms of a truce. So convinced were the Welsh of the good faith of De Braose they observed the custom of the day by leaving their weapons in an anteroom before entering the hall to dine. They had hardly sat down when De Braose, with false piety, exclaimed, 'Let this be done in the name of the Lord', which was a pre-arranged signal for his armed soldiers to rush into the hall. In no time the place was a shambles, the reed-covered floor soaking up the blood of seventy-five Welshmen. The treacherous Lord of Abergavenny then led his butchers to Castle Arnold (which stood on a site already visited) and murdered Sytsyllt's wife Anharad, Cadwaladr his infant son, and other members of his family.

About seven or so years afterwards the Welsh took their revenge, and in doing so showed that they knew something about strategic warfare. They let it be known of their intention to attack the castle on a certain night, causing the Norman garrison to stand at their posts, inflicting on them a long and bitterly cold winter vigil. Nothing happened, so the cold and weary soldiers, cursing the cowardly Welsh, stumbled back to their beds. As soon as they were asleep the Welsh attacked the castle and avenged the massacre of their comrades. De Braose escaped, but his luck ran out when, after a quarrel with King John, he was stripped of his land and titles, then chased out of the country to exile and a lonely death in France.

Fate decreed that subsequent heirs to the lordship of Abergavenny would suffer ill-fortune; one was only seventeen when he was killed in a tournament; another died after being struck by a stone from a battle-sling, and William de Braose's grandson was hanged from a tree in North Wales by Prince Llywelyn because of the Norman's intrigue with his wife. The grandeur of the castle ended in 1404 after Owain Glyndwr had battered it and the town. In 1645, as part of a 'scorched earth policy', it was rendered unusable for his enemies by King Charles I who, about this time, passed through the town on his way to stay at Raglan Castle.

After building the castle Hamelin de Balun found further work for his masons in building the Priory Church of St Mary. Time, and the vandalism of the Ironside soldiers caused little of the original building to survive, but the splendid monuments in a side chapel will interest the antiquary and historian. Because of their historical importance they are listed as follows,

EVA DE BRAOSE, daughter of William Marshall, Earl of Pembroke, wife of William de Braose, Lord of Abergavenny. Died 1246.

GEORGE DE CANTELUPE, Lord of Abergavenny, son of William. Born 1253 Died 1273.

LAWRENCE DE HASTINGS, Lord of Abergavenny. Died 1248.

SIR WILLIAM DE HASTINGS, half-brother to Lawrence. Died 1349.

SIR WILLIAM AP THOMAS, ancestor of all the noble Herbert families, and the father of the first Earl of Pembroke. Died 1446. Also Gwladys, his wife, who died in 1454.

SIR RICHARD HERBERT OF COLDBROOK, beheaded at Banbury 1459, and Margaret his wife.

SIR RICHARD HERBERT OF EWYAS, natural son of Sir William Herbert, and ancestor of the Earls of Pembroke and Caernarfon, and the Marquis of Bute. Died 1510.

In time the town became better known for its trades than the martial activities of former years. In 1600 it was described as being 'wealthy and thriving'. It sold the best quality Welsh flannel, and part of Flannel Street, where the weavers and merchants worked, still exists. Due to sharp practice of some of the traders this industry declined, and the manufacture of flannel went to Montgomeryshire. Next the town gained a reputation for making fine wigs and shoes. Nowadays its fortunes are linked with agriculture and market activities and, in season, it is a profitable tourist centre.

Take a walk around the town, avoiding the Tuesday market day when the streets are crowded, and you will find a great deal to interest you. In Cross Street an ancient archway adjacent to the market entrance is said to have once given access to a medieval tilt-yard, and alongside the market building the street is one which once led to Traitors Gate. Many of the side streets are lined with houses of Georgian times, having exquisite pilastered and pedimented doorways of Adam style. Then there are the old inns. In Flannel Street is the Hen and Chicken, said to have been a favourite haunt of the bibulous tramp-poet W.H. Davies; he is supposed to have written the following lines when he visited the inn,

O what a merry world I see
Before me through a quart of ale.

In Cross Street is The George, but perhaps a more accurate name for this inn would be 'The Two Georges', for its sign shows George Washington on one side and the red-bearded Irish playwright, George Bernard Shaw on the other. Behind the King's Arms in Neville Street is part of the medieval town wall which ran between several gateways. In the same street is a shop which was once the Cow Inn, easily recognised by the line of brightly coloured bovine heads supporting the eaves soffit.

114

The mountains above Abergavenny provide some fine viewpoints. One is this view of the Black Mountains from the summit of the Sugar Loaf mountain.

The ridgeway tracks of the Black Mountains are easily reached from Abergavenny, and provide interesting walks.

Below the horned heads the window openings have moulded frames which give an indication of the historical richness of the town. The frames are decorated with Tudor Roses and the arms of a famous Silurian family – the Vaughans of Tretower Court, an ancient manor house between Abergavenny and Brecon.

CHAPTER EIGHT

From Abergavenny to the Radnorshire Hills

A few miles south-west of Abergavenny, between Llanfoist and Govilon, a road leaves the A465, crossing the Abergavenny – Brecon canal to climb the Blorenge mountain to Blaenavon, a place where an industry started centuries ago and continued into the 20th century. Here, and among the surrounding hills, the Silurians set up primitive forges to manufacture weapons to use in their long fight against the Romans, Saxon and Norman invaders. In the 19th century caves in nearby mountains were used as hiding places by the Chartist rebels, and as manufacturies where they could make pikes and other weapons to aid them in a fight to obtain fair treatment from the avaricious ironmasters. The story of those times, and of the Chartist uprising, is graphically described by Alexander Cordell in his book, *Rape of the Fair Country*.

The forging of metals and the building of iron and steelworks might not have happened here if an edict of Queen Elizabeth I had been obeyed. She decreed 'that as ironworks are great destroyers of timber, their erection, within certain limits, shall be prohibited'. The mountains around and above Blaenavon were quarried and blasted to supply minerals and metals for the industrialisation of Britain. Huge profits were made by the ironmasters and, until they revolted, a hazardous life of toil and poverty was the lot of the workers. When coal replaced charcoal to fire the furnaces in the 1840s a new and even more profitable industry grew in the valleys of South Wales.

Interest in industrial archaeology has increased, and at Blaenavon buildings and equipment used have been restored and preserved as milestones of the 18th and 19th centuries' industrial revolution. You can see two of the huge blast furnaces, and near it the small cottages which the ironmasters built for the workers. The coal industry is represented by the Big Pit which has one of the oldest mine-shafts in Wales, and this is now open for the public to visit. Remains of old tramroads can be found, and also the incline along which trams ran the ironstone, coal and quarried stone down the mountain to the canal wharf at Llanfoist. Blaenavon street names evoke memories – Lime-kiln Terrace, Furnace Row, The Bunkers and Hall Pit are some of them. The earth is scarred and covered with slag heaps of this dismal age, visual and bitter memorials of the past.

From Abergavenny to the Radnorshire Hills

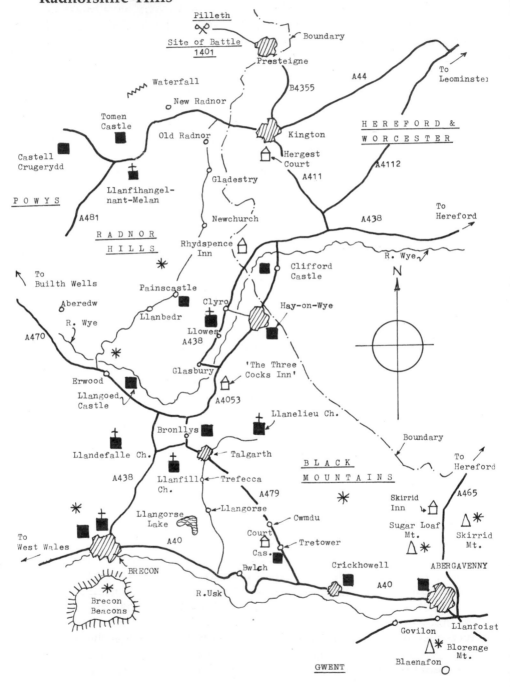

Pilleth
Site of Battle 1401
Boundary
Presteigne
Waterfall
B4355
A44
To Leominster
New Radnor
Tomen Castle
Old Radnor
Kington
HEREFORD & WORCESTER
Castell Crugerydd
Hergest Court
A4112
POWYS
Llanfihangel-nant-Melan
Gladestry
A411
A481
Newchurch
A438
To Hereford
RADNOR HILLS
Rhydspence Inn
Clifford Castle
R. Wye
N
To Builth Wells
Painscastle
Clyro
Hay-on-Wye
Aberedw
Llanbedr
R. Wye
Llowes
A470
A438
Glasbury
'The Three Cocks Inn'
Erwood
Llangoed Castle
A4053
Llanelieu Ch.
Bronllys
Boundary
Llandefalle Ch.
Talgarth
BLACK MOUNTAINS
To Hereford
A438
Llanfillo Ch.
Trefecca
A479
Skirrid Inn
A465
Llangorse Lake
Llangorse
Cwmdu
Sugar Loaf Mt.
Skirrid Mt.
To West Wales
A40
Court Cas.
Tretower
BRECON
Crickhowell
ABERGAVENNY
Brecon Beacons
Bwlch
R. Usk
A40
Govilon
Llanfoist
Blorenge Mt.
Blaenafon
GWENT

From the Blorenge the views are extensive, but not more so than from the Sugar Loaf mountain on the north side of the Usk Valley. From the A40 trunk road Pentre Lane provides the easiest route to the mountain summit. When a car park is reached a grassy track leads to the top of the mountain – a walk of about thirty to forty minutes. The narrow elongated summit accounts for the changing shape of the mountain when seen from different parts of Gwent. From north and south it is seen as a flat table-land, but from east and west as a cone, shaped very much like Mount Fujiyama in Japan. Views from the summit are extensive, and if the day is clear the drifting clouds, casting translucent shadows in the deep hollows of the Black Mountains, make the prospect variable. To the east is the long sharply defined ridge of Skirrid Fawr, and across the Usk valley the bulk of the Blorenge spreads a shadow over the land.

Next along the A40 is Crickhowell where the Usk is a fisherman's paradise; a fact confirmed by the inn sign of The Bear which shows a brown bear with a large salmon in his paw, and he also holds a fishing rod. Nowadays the town is fairly quiet, much more so than when it rivalled Abergavenny for fine Welsh flannel and shoes, two trades mentioned by Smollet in his book *Humphrey Clinker* which gives an account of the town's activities. Situated between the Usk and the foothills of the Penalltmawr mountain range Crickhowell is in a perfect setting. The Silures of this area were always quick to defend their land and homes, a fact realised by Bernard de Newmarch when he marched on the town. Peace was often restored when a Norman lord married a Welsh princess, and more often than not such an alliance was motivated by political reasons, but it is hard to believe that De Newmarch married the grand-daughter of the great Llywelyn for reasons other than romantic. Straddling the road between Abergavenny and Brecon the town suffered fire and slaughter from Norman and Welsh. When the castle was held by the Pauncfotes they strengthened it and the outer defences, but not enough to prevent Owain Glyndwr, on his way to attack Abergavenny, battering the fortress walls and setting fire to the town.

Where the Usk river touches the road near Glen Usk Park there is a choice of routes; the A40 will take you through Bwlch to Brecon, and then set you on the way to West Wales. From the road junction the A479 runs between the western flank of the Black Mountains and their outlying hills to the valley of the Middle Wye. When the Normans, after taking Abergavenny, reached this spot they must have paused, for the information brought by their scouts would have warned them that a hot reception awaited them from the Welsh at Bwlch. *Bwlch* is the Welsh word for pass, and the narrow defile between Buckland Hill and the southern tip of Mynydd Llangorse is nothing less. They would have also

From the Usk valley a road runs up the Blorenge mountain to the industrial area of north-west Gwent. In the distance is the Sugar Loaf mountain.

The canal between Abergavenny and Brecon is now a quiet waterway, passing through some of the most beautiful scenery in South Wales.

learned that those who escaped the arrows and spears of the Welsh would meet opposition from another force pouring out of Castell Blaenllynfi just the other side of the pass.

Romans and Normans would have paused here to take stock and plan the next stage of advance. It is possible that they would have made a feint attack to keep the guardians of the *bwlch* occupied, sending a larger number of troops to find a less formidable gateway. They found an excellent back-door entry through another pass at the head of Cwm Sorgwm. This, of course, is a conjectural but feasible theory, so as our journey is to explore the Marchlands of Wales this back-door route is the one to take.

A short way along the A479 is Tretower, a small village taking its name from the high tower of the Norman castle, so that an acceptable name would be 'The Town of the Tower'. Tretower Court adjoins the old castle, a home according to Leland as 'the fair place of Henry Vehan . . . an excellent Perpendicular house on a large scale, modified by certain attention to defence'. It is considered to be one of the finest examples of a medieval manor house in Britain. The castle rises from a mound which was first fortified by the Welsh chieftain Bleddin. After he was killed in battle in about 1090 Bernard de Newmarch commenced building a tower-keep above a triangular courtyard. Through marriage between Welsh and Norman families it eventually became the home of poets and brave soldiers – a family which became known as the Vaughans of Tretower.

About three miles away a red telephone box marks the entry point into the Cwm Sorgwm valley. The cwm ends at a narrow gap between Mynydd Troed and Mynydd Llangorse; both summits are easily climbed, but the latter one requires less effort. From the summit you will have expansive views; eastwards, the long ranging mountain of Penalltmawr, the highest peak of Waun Fach to the north, and in the south the ridge ends at Pen Cerrig Calch. Northwards are the hills of Powys, and the sun-gilded Wye passing in great loops through the pastures of Herefordshire. The intimacy of the western view is magical – Llangorse Lake lies at the foot of the mountain, and across the Vale of Usk rise the majestic heights of the Brecon Beacons.

A lane from the cwm leads down to Llangorse Lake, the largest one in South Wales. Legend claims that a Roman city lies in the depths of the lake, and records tell of people who insist that they have seen dim outlines of the Roman Loventium beneath the waters. Gerald, the historian, who loved embellishing a legend, especially one which allows a prince of Wales to discomfort a Norman invader, wrote as follows,

It is an ancient saying in Wales, that if the natural prince of the country, coming to this lake, shall order the birds to sing, they will

Tretower Castle guards two mountain passes – one through Bwlch to West and Mid Wales, and a Black Mountain valley pass to Talgarth and the Wye Valley.

Tretower Court, adjacent to the castle, is considered to be a good example of a fortified manor house. It was the home of soldiers and poets.

immediately obey him. . . . Gruffydd, falling on his knees towards the east, as if he had been about to engage in battle, with his eyes and hands uplifted to heaven he thus spoke openly: Almighty God, Who knowest all things, declare here this day Thy power. If Thou has caused me to descend lineally from the natural princes of Wales, I command these birds in Thy name to declare it: and immediately the birds, beating the waters with their wings, began to cry and proclaim him.

This is supposed to have happened in the reign of King Henry I, when Gruffydd, the son of Rhys ap Tudor, passed by the lake in the company of the Earl of Hereford and Lord FitzJohn of Ewyas.

The lake and district may have been a place of habitation several thousand years ago, at a time when people felt safer living in huts supported on stakes driven into the bed of the lake. About sixty years ago a primitive dug-out canoe, fashioned from a single tree-trunk, was recovered from the lake. Maybe it was once used by the ancient lake-dwellers, or those who came to fish in the lake from the hut circles on the summit of Mynydd Troed.

North of Llangorse is Trefecca the birthplace of Howell Harris who became known as the Luther of Wales. He was born here in 1714, son of a poor farmer. After studying at Oxford he became an evangelic preacher, and founder of the Methodist Church in Wales. The established church disapproved of his teachings, and he was often attacked, but despite this he had very many followers. One of his strongest supporters was Selina, Countess of Huntingdon, and when he died in 1773 over 20,000 people followed his coffin from Trefecca to a grave at Talgarth.

Its position in front of a 1,000 feet high spur of the Black Mountains accounts for the name of Talgarth, for it means 'the Town in front of the Hill'. During the 19th century the small town having monthly markets and eight fair days a year must have been a busy place, so the claim that the Black Lion Inn, at the corner of Regent Street, is one of 21 coaching inns which existed during the 19th century is probably true. Talgarth was once the capital of Brycheinog, (Breconshire) and was ruled by Brychan. The parish church is dedicated to Brychan's daughter Gwendoline who was murdered by the Saxons. Inside the 13th century church is a memorial to Howell Harris, claiming that he was 'a faithful member of the Church of England'. A claim that he had been a faithful member of the Methodist Church of Wales would have been preferred by Harris and his followers.

Talgarth provides access to three of the most interesting churches in the Marches – Llanelieu, Llanfillo and Llandefalle. To reach the first of them, Llanelieu, you pass a building claiming to have been a house of

View of the Black Mountains from Cwm Sorgwm Pass near Talgarth.

Late afternoon bathers, Llangorse Lake. In the distance are the Brecon Beacons.

rest for pilgrims on their way from Llanthony Priory to Brecon. A stone in the porch is dated 1676, and there are faint traces of a Latin inscription. The small church is primitive, the most interesting feature being inside – a roughly fashioned rood screen dating from the middle years of the 14th century. Wishing to be left in peace the natives of these parts made sure not to offend any participants in the Wars of the Roses. To please those who fought under the sign of the Red Rose they decorated the screen with red roses, but when Yorkist forces were sighted the colour was quickly changed to white.

The churches at Llanfillo and Llandefalle are found on hillsides west of Talgarth, both easily reached from the A470 road to Brecon. Inside the former is a font which may have been fashioned before the Conquest, but the most interesting feature here is the magnificent rood screen and loft. The panels of the loft are carved with figures of the apostles, and the Virgin is shown seated beneath the archway of a castle. Above is a cross bearing the crucified figure of Christ. The date of the lovely screen is about 1500, and although a careful restoration was carried out in 1925, most of it is in an original state. Llandefalle church also has a screen contemporary with the 15th century building. It is decorated with carved crocketted crosses and bosses displaying the Tudor emblem of a rose.

The road from Talgarth soon joins the A438 Brecon to Hay-on-Wye road, and here we turn right to find a convenient spot to cross the Wye. About two miles away stands the old coaching inn of The Three Cocks. There is a saying in these parts that 'once a Welshman goes through Bwlch he never returns'. Eight or nine hundred years ago this saying could also have applied to any foreigner from across the Wye making his way westwards past the site of the Three Cocks. Today it is different, for the old inn now welcomes all who make it their headquarters when fishing the Llynfi and the Wye, and equal hospitality is offered to Welsh and English.

Years ago the inns, except those which were guesthouses for passing pilgrims, were not safe to spend a night in. Their landlords were often in partnership with the local highwayman, giving him information when they saw a careless customer with a well-filled purse. These hostelries were neither clean nor godly. John Taylor, a 17th century poet with a gift for composing descriptive (but sometimes bawdy) prose and verse, once wrote of his discomfort in a country inn. He wrote, 'I was furiously assaulted by an Ethiopian army of fleas . . . I laid so manfully about me that I made more than 500 *mortus est* . . . I rubbed them between my finger and thumb, and they were so plump and mellow that they would squash to pieces like boiled peas'. On finding better accommodation he wrote the following verse,

An early 14th-century rood screen and loft at Llanelieu near Talgarth.

In contrast to the Llanelieu screen the one at Llanfillo, of 200 years later, is magnificent and one of the treasures of Wales.

From nasty rooms that never felt brooms,
From excrements and all bad scents,
From children bawling and caterwauling,
From grunts of hogs and barking of dogs,
And from biting of fleas I found ease'.

In time the inns and their keepers became respectable. The inns becoming cleaner and much more comfortable. Their stone-flagged floors were kept swept and sanded, the large ceiling beams were gaily decorated with brasses and old pewter work, and succulent flitches hung on hooks to titillate the customer's palate. Coaching days brought prosperity, and the Pickwickian scenes of those colourful times are often used to illustrate our cards of Christmas greeting. Today's inns set out to be convivial, and picturesque signs often suggest the friendly atmosphere that may be found inside.

The Wye can be crossed at Glasbury, where the riverside scenery is at its rural best, or at Hay-on-Wye. On the opposite bank from Hay is Clyro. From here Trehearne Vaughan rode to meet De Braose who dragged him bound to the tail of a horse to a shameful death at Brecon, an act which caused Prince Gwenwynwyn of Powys to vow that he would 'sweep De Braose's land as clean as the palm of his hand'. He led an attack on the Norman's lair at Painscastle, and may have succeeded had his rival Gruffydd ap Rhys not helped the Normans defeat the avenging Welsh forces.

Nearby is Llowes where the church contains an ancient cross thought to have been fashioned from a stone brought down from the mountain by St Meilig. This supposition is more feasible than that it was a pebble which Moll Walbee,(Maud de Valerie) wife of de Braose, took from her shoe and flung from Abergavenny to Llowes churchyard. However, it is known as 'Moll's Stone', but it is not known who carved pagan symbols on it, but it must have been someone who lived here several centuries before the Marcher Lords came here during the closing years of the 11th century.

Glasbury, the next Wye-side village, is now a far more peaceful place than when the Saxons settled here and gave it the name of Gwladys Burh. Gwladys was the daughter of Brychan Brycheinog, a chieftain who ruled in these parts. A modern mansion is known as Maesllwch Castle, and near it is Maesyronen Congregational Chapel, the oldest Non-Conformist place of worship in Wales; Oliver Cromwell is supposed to have preached in it. The village is at the southern tip of the Radnorshire Hills, an area with an intricate network of lanes, most of them branching from one main road (the B4594) which runs north-east from Erwood towards Old Radnor. It is an area worth exploring, but a detailed map is essential.

From Glasbury the road soon becomes a narrow lane, passing through Llanstephan to Erwood. Across the Wye is Llyswen, a name supposed to mean 'White Palace'; the history of the opulent mansion known as Llangoed Castle confirms this. Inside the mansion two 17th century paintings show a great white castle where, according to a Welsh legend, a prince once lived. To atone for the evil life he led the story is that he gave his fine home to the bishopric of Llandaff near Cardiff. The present 'castle', built in 1911, was designed by the late Sir Clough Williams-Ellis, the imaginative architect who created Portmeirion in North Wales.

Erwood means 'The Ford'. The Welsh called it Y Rhyd, an appropriate name for here the Welsh drovers', after crossing the Cambrian Mountains of Mid-Wales, forded the Wye to drive their cattle to the English markets. Near here is our starting point for exploration of the Radnor Hills. The road we are about to take, the B4594, has a branch which leads to Aberedw, a place where Prince Llywelyn, the last Welsh Prince of Wales, found refuge in a hermit's cave the night before he was slain in a miserable skirmish at Cilmery near Builth Wells. A simple obelisk is all that remains to remind us of his last stand in the fight to free Wales from Anglo-Norman oppression.

The Radnorshire Hills

From Erwood the road on the opposite bank of the Wye climbs into a land where De Braose, and others like him, sought to harry the Welsh. The road runs a switchback course over the hills to Painscastle, a place already written about – one of violent history where fortifications once stood to provide a base for barons and kings in their war against Prince Llywelyn Fawr. This hill country is sparsely populated, its activities being mainly agricultural leaves the air free from industrial pollution. It has been described as 'a labyrinth of moorlands and valleys – a region almost unknown'. The writer A.G. Bradley referred to it as a 'broken but delightful Arcady'. After running between Clytha Hill and Bryngwyn Hill the road reaches Newchurch. This is an attractive village and one which King Charles I found friendly when he requested a glass of milk from one of the villagers.

Next, almost touching the border, is Gladestry; in fact it is near two borders – the ancient one of King Offa and the present delineated one. You can climb to the western end of Hergest ridge and walk along the Offa's Dyke footpath to the outskirts of Kington, and then along easier contours to cross back into Wales again at Burfa Camp. The surrounding countryside is worth exploring, but if you have to hurry on a northward road soon reaches Old Radnor. This was once the home of Harold Godwinson who failed to prevent the Norman hordes landing at

Hastings in 1066. Harold all but destroyed Old Radnor, replacing it with a town which became known as New Radnor. *New*, perhaps, is a misnomer, for it is mentioned in the Domesday Book. King Edward I found little need to strengthen the defences thrown up by the early Lords Marchers, but it is recorded that King John destroyed a *stone* castle – one which was rebuilt by King Henry III, and then reduced to a shapeless ruin by Owain Glyndwr in 1401.

When King Charles I sought shelter he had to make do with a less grand place than a castle to rest in. He is said to have stayed at a poor inn then known as The Bush. He was not well received, and little effort was made to make him comfortable. One who was with him wrote,

> The king laid in a poor low chamber, and my Lord of Lindsay and others by the kitchen fire in hay. He was given a scrawny pullet and a small piece of cheese to eat, and before the King had eaten it the poor woman of the house entered the room and asked if he had finished with the cheese – for the gentlemen without desired it.

King Charles, still hungry, and now in a bad temper, suggested that the inn should henceforth be called 'The *Beggars* Bush'.

Running west the A44 reaches Llanfihangel-nant-Melan where the church stands within a circle of yews which replaces one of stone. Between a mountain stream and the tip of Radnor Forest is a site marked on the map as Tomen Castle, and among the hills you may find Castell Crugerydd, originally called Crug Eryr, 'the Eagles Crag'. A branch road off the A44 leads to Builth Wells and the valley of the Wye.

Other interesting places are easily accessible from New and Old Radnor. North of the latter is Walton Court of early cruck construction. The poet Wordsworth, who often visited this area of the Welsh border country, had friends who lived in a nearby farmhouse. The Welsh had a fortification here to deal with the forces of Harold when they came across the ramparts and ditches of Offa's Dyke which went south from here over Bradnor Hill to the outskirts of Kington.

Not far away, between the Lugg and a tributary stream, is a spot marked by a small black cross on the map as Pilleth. It was here that an army of Glyndwr, led by Rhys Gethin, defeated the army of Edmund Mortimer. At this time the Lugg was a Welsh river, and was called the Llugwy. Mounds in the riverside meadows are said to cover the bodies of the English dead. The slaughter of the English soldiers on a summer day in 1401 was terrible, for the long-bows of the Welsh archers decimated the men of Mortimer, for more than 1,000 of them met their death that day at Pilleth. To be killed outright by a clean bow-shot was merciful, for those less fortunate were hacked to pieces, and according to Shakespeare's account of the battle the Welsh women-folk inflicted shocking indignities on the corpses of the English. Shakespeare wrote,

> . . . the noble Mortimer,
> Leading the men of Herefordshire to fight,
> Against the irregular and wild Glendower –
> Was, by the rude hands of that Welshman, taken,
> And a thousand of his people butcher'd;
> Such beastly, shameless transformation,
> By these Welshwomen done, as may not be,
> Without much shame, retold or spoken of.

Edmund Mortimer was spared, but Glyndwr held him a prisoner until he agreed to marry one of his daughters. Another historic battle claimed to have taken place in this area was that in which Caractacus made his last stand against the Roman army led by Scapula. From historians' descriptions of the site of battle the site on a hill called Caer Caradoc is a feasible place – but so are others in different parts of the Celtic borderland.

West of Pilleth is Monaughty where a monastery once stood. There are no remains of such a building now, unless a church built on a nearby mound, of 13th century origin, was once a part of it. To the north, almost on the Welsh border, is another mound which is supposed to have supported the keep of a castle built by Cogfran Gawr, the father of Guinevere who married King Arthur there. That the ancient mound was once part of a Mortimer stronghold is a feasible concept, but other stories connected with it can only be considered as interesting legends. About one mile south-east of the mound is the border town of Knighton which stands on the line of Offa's Dyke.

The Welsh called Knighton Trefclawdd, which means 'the Town on the Dyke', a more acceptable name than one which the Saxons, who had a settlement there, probably gave it. The Welsh threw the Saxon invaders out in 1052, but about fifteen years later they were ousted by the Normans who built a mounded fortress to the east. The Welsh, as usual, provided a logical name when they called it Bryn-y-Castell. The town of Knighton, set amid low hills is very attractive, and on a market day a busy place. The streets are steep and narrow – in fact the upper part of the town is known as 'The Narrows'.

Presteigne, another of the larger towns in this section of the Welsh borderland, is squeezed between the B4362 and the river Lugg, and is only just in Wales. Its history starts in pre-Conquest days, for tradition claims that Caractacus made his battle plans here before marching away to meet the Romans. The wide streets contain many beautiful buildings; one of the largest, the Radnorshire Arms, was not always an inn, for in the 17th century it was the home of Sir Christopher Hatton, a member of

Queen Elizabeth's Court. Apart from suffering attacks by Welsh and English the town bore other afflictions. Between 1551 and 1636 a series of plagues decimated the population and was responsible for closing down the woollen trade. This and other sad memories are ones which the people of the town would like to forget, particularly an incident which happened in 1805. In that year the uncaring narrow-minded people witnessed the hanging of 17 year old Mary Morgan for murdering her new-born child. It is thought that the cowardly father of her child was the judge who sentenced her. The spot where she was hanged is known as Gallows Lane, and a tombstone in the churchyard marks her place of burial. Proof of the town's antiquity is evident in the name of another lane; this is called Harpers Lane, after a family who lived there in 1338.

Presteigne and other nearby places have lurid stories connected with the supernatural. It was in the spacious parish church that the evil spirit of Black Vaughan of Hergest Court was laid – how this was done is told on page 63. About a mile away stand the ruins of a 17th century mansion, built on the site of a castle owned by Sir John Cornewall who fought at Agincourt, and afterwards married the sister of King Henry V. Two members of this family have tombs in the church; Geoffrey, who died in 1335, and Anne who died at the castle, when only 17, in 1671. An old rhyme tells of a mistress of the mansion (it is known as Stapleton Court) who, so it is rumoured, was murdered by her steward. She haunts the ruins clad in a long black gown and wears blue shoes. The rhyme, which seems incomplete, goes,

Lady Bluefoot, all in black,
Silver buttons down her back,
Harrigoshee! Harrigoshee!
Lock the cupboard and take the key.

The meaning of the word 'Harrigoshee' is uncertain; perhaps it is one used to frighten away the ghost?

Kington is the last place we shall visit on this part of the journey through the Marches. Situated at the eastern end of Hergest Ridge it also touches Offa's Dyke; in fact it is just on the English side of the dyke. When it was owned by the people on the other side of the dyke it had a different name, but when, in 1055, Harold drove the Welsh away he renamed the town Kings Town, a name near enough to the present Kington. As a border town it was fought over, so the church, like other border ones, has a detached tower, a last place of refuge in the event of a raid. The Welsh origin of Kington is confirmed by the tombs inside the church. One belongs to Thomas Vaughan of Tretower who met his death at Banbury in 1469. He lies in company with his Amazon spouse,

In the 17th century the Radnorshire Arms at Presteigne was the home of a favoured member of the Court of Queen Elizabeth I.

(whom we have already met on page 63) 'Elin Gethin the Terrible', who shot an arrow through the heart of her brother's murderer.

Other famous names are connected with Kington. John Wesley preached in the church on August 15th 1746; Sarah Siddons and Stephen Kemble, who was born in the town, acted there. Relatives of Wordsworth owned a nearby house, and Sir Edward Elgar was a visitor. Sir John Abel, 'the King's Carpenter,' was responsible for the design of the local Grammar School which was built in 1662. This fine building was founded by Margaret Vaughan of Hergest Court, she was the wife of that famous Elizabethan sea captain and terror of the Spaniards, Sir John Hawkins.

From Hereford to Leominster and Ludlow

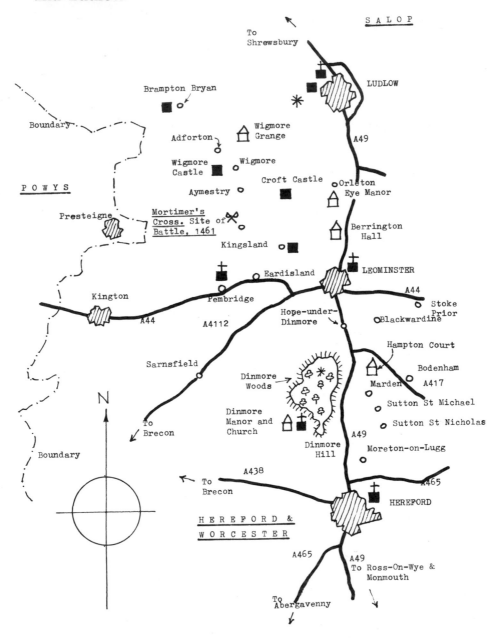

CHAPTER NINE

From Hereford to Leominster and Ludlow

Our previous journeys have led us to the outskirts of Hereford, a city which we shall now explore. Its origin is ancient, created on a site of important strategic value. People probably settled there long before the Romans established themselves, constructing the first stone buildings with materials brought from the ruins of Magna Castra.

A legend tells of how Tintern Abbey owes its origin to an act of repentance (page 26). The foundations of Hereford's cathedral were also laid as proof of true penance for an evil deed. This happened when Ethelbert, the Christian King of East Anglia, was murdered by his prospective father-in-law Offa. Some claim that it was Offa's wife who was responsible for the murder, but whatever the truth is a repentant Offa raised the walls of a church to enshrine his victim and perpetuate his name.

In Offa's time Hereford was a garrison town, and called by the Saxons Hen-fford which means 'War Ford' or 'Army Ford'. Offa raised his famous dyke to the west, and at about the same time walled in the town with a similar ditch and earthen bank. Within the area enclosed by these early ramparts, later replaced in stone, is the general layout of the streets as planned before the Norman Conquest.

Throughout the centuries, up to 1645 when the town was disturbed by the fluctuating fortunes of the Civil War, Hereford was hardly ever a peaceful place. Situated in the Middle Marches it was in the centre of the long struggle between the Welsh and Normans, and the castle built by Harold of Hastings was taken and rebuilt when the Conqueror made his kinsman, William FitzOsbern, the Earl of Hereford soon after the Conquest. After this the Earl, and his bishop, Robert Losinga, initiated the building of the present cathedral, a building which is mainly of the early Norman period. A description of the cathedral's architecture, in detail, might prove indigestible, so this is best left to the various excellent guides published by the Dean and Cathedral Chapter.

Is, or was, Hereford in Wales? This depends on the period of history under discussion, and also on the claimed nationality of the person asked to reply to such a question. Centuries ago the customs and ideas here were Welsh, and in official documents 'Hereford in Wales' was a common usage. Many places have Welsh names, and in 1885 the

To the people of Hereford this is affectionately known as 'the Old House.' It is all that remains of the Guild Houses which stood in High Town in 1612.

Magistrate's Clerk was appointed because he was able to speak Welsh. Study of the town's ancient charters, many retained in the Town Hall, will be of interest, even if not conclusive, on this point.

Studying the buildings of the town makes one uncomfortably aware that over-modernisation may, if not quickly restrained, cause the town to lose its character. Cellars of many buildings, particularly of the pubs, have stonework and arched vaulting built in the 13th century. Sections of the medieval town walls and traces of gateways have been preserved, and a great deal is left to prove that they withstood the battering of cannons during the sieges of the Civil War.

In the centre of High Town, now facing a pedestrianised area, is all that is left of 'Butchers Row', the timbered Guild houses which stood here in 1612. The house left standing is affectionately called 'the Old House', and now serves as a museum – its panelled rooms containing the furniture used in the early days of the 17th century. Not far away is another timbered house of the same period. When Littlewoods built a new store they carefully *removed* the house to stand, wrapped in a protective covering, in the centre of High Town, then when the builders were ready it was moved on rollers back to its original position to form part of the new store.

From High Town an alley leads to Booth Hall, an even older building according to records of 1392 which state that Richard III gave permission for the erection of '. . . a hall wherein to hold pleas'. Further proof of its antiquity was found in 1919 when masonry collapsed to reveal roof timbers dating back to the closing years of the 13th century. It served as an assembly hall until, in 1780, part of it became an inn. One of the first landlords was Tom Winter, better known as Tom Spring who in 1825 was champion pugilist of England. In Widemarsh Street are alms-houses built in 1614 by Sir Thomas Coningsby to provide comfortable quarters for aged soldiers, and in a field behind are the remains of a Dominican Priory and a Preaching Cross of the same period. There are ancient churches too, St Peter's and All Saints being among them.

The names of famous people are associated with the town. Owen Tudor, after capture at the battle of Mortimer's Cross, met his death on the block at a public execution in the market place. The deposed favourite of Edward II was also a captive, leaving this world after his suspension from a 50 ft high gallows. In Gwynne Street a plaque marks the birth-place of Nell who left Hereford for London to walk the boards of a theatre in Drury Lane – before walking the soft-carpeted floor of a royal bedchamber. Perhaps Nell obtained the idea for the Chelsea Pensioners Home, which she persuaded her royal master to build, from the ones she saw as a child in Widemarsh Street. Another plaque on a wall in Widemarsh Street informs you that David Garrick was born there in 1717. The famous Kembles also lived in Hereford, and David Cox,

The River Wye and the medieval bridge at Hereford. In the background is the Cathedral.

The almshouses in Widemarsh Street were built for war veterans in 1614 by Sir Thomas Coningsby.

who painted many local scenes, taught art at the Cathedral School. A tall column rising from the centre of Castle Green was erected in honour of Lord Nelson, a Freeman of the town.

The first castle in Hereford was built about fourteen years before the Conquest, and is claimed by historians to be one of the earliest built within a town. When William FitzOsbern marched across the Wye he enlarged and improved the castle defences. After demolition by Colonel Birch in the Civil War nothing is left except an embankment and part of the moat which is now known as Castle Pool.

This is but a brief description and history of the city of Hereford and what may be seen there, although there are bound to be omissions, but lack of space does not allow any further information.

Our route, the A49, runs due north through the Marcher borderland to Leominster and Ludlow, two towns which played important parts in the long history of our country. About four miles from the centre of Hereford is Moreton-on-Lugg from where you can cross the River Lugg to Sutton St Michael and Sutton St Nicholas. Near here King Offa had his palace, the scene of Ethelbert's murder. North of the two Suttons is Marden which has a church on the bank of the Lugg. Offa, who had buried the body of Ethelbert near the river in an unmarked grave became afraid when he was told of strange lights appearing over the martyr's burial place – so he arranged for reburial at Hereford. A spring marks the spot of the first burial, and when a church was built there it was constructed over the spring which was enclosed and used as a well. Inside Marden church is an interesting brass memorial to Margaret Chute. Her early 17th century home of Wisteston Court is still occupied, and is one of many pictorial farms and cottages in the Herefordshire countryside.

Soon after leaving Moreton-on-Lugg the A49 winds up Dinmore Hill to a convenient car park. The wooded area on top of the hill is called Queenswood Arboretum and Park, so named to mark the coronation of Queen Elizabeth II. This rich woodland, covering an area of nearly 200 acres, was held by the Crown until it was sold to the Coningsby family in the 16th century, but it is now in the management of the County Council of Herefordshire. Green avenues have been cut through the trees giving easy access to picnic areas; one, called Jubilee Walk, leads to a ridge from where the visitor can look across the Herefordshire landscape – to the saw-toothed outlines of the Malvern Hills and the Black Mountains of Wales. On the ridge is an ingenious device indicating the direction of the main features of an extensive panoramic view. Fallow deer, foxes and grey squirrels can be seen in various parts of the wood.

From Queenswood the A49 curves between the trees to the bottom of Dinmore Hill, the road becoming less steep when it reaches the small

A Springtime walk in Dinmore Woods. From a ridge there are expansive panoramic views over the Herefordshire landscape.

hamlet of Hope-under-Dinmore. Near here a lane leads to the entrance gateway of Dinmore Manor, an ancient house with a small chapel once used by the Knights Hospitaller. The chapel, in fact, is older than the house as it dates back to the 12th century, the manor house being built about two hundred years later. The glass in the east window of the chapel is alive with colour, showing Christ surrounded by his disciples and saints, and a tablet informs you that Thomas Dunemore founded the chapel in 1163. It was not always the case but here the Knights Hospitaller, unlike the Templars, were well thought of, and this is confirmed by the words painted on the tablet,

The knights are dust
Their swords are rust;
Their souls are with
The saints, we trust.

From Hope-under-Dinmore another road leaves the A49 across the Lugg soon to pass the finest mansion in the county. Hampton Court was founded in 1434 by Sir Ronald Lenthall from ransom money he extracted, as was the custom at that time, from French nobles he captured at Agincourt. In time the mansion, largely rebuilt in 1700, became the home of the Viscounts of Hereford. There exists a strange legend concerning a painting inside the house of a dog known as the Coningsby Hound. It is said that if the painting is removed the owner of the house will meet with a violent death. When Lord Hereford bought the house in 1772 he evidently decided not to tempt providence, so made arrangements that the picture of the hound was left to avoid fulfillment of the legend.

After reaching a picturesque inn called England's Gate you will soon reach Bodenham, a small village of timbered houses lying close to the Lugg. There are two ancient houses here; one, built of mellowed stone and timber dates from the 14th century, with additions built in the 17th century. Not far away is Broadfield Court which also dates from the 14th century. The windows of the house are interesting for they mark the progress of the development of Broadfield Court from its earliest days to Victorian times.

About one mile beyond the junction of the A417 with the A49 a lane from the latter road leads to the village of Stoke Prior, a place which takes its name from the 14th century priory situated about three miles away. Nearby is Blackwardine, known in Roman times as Black-Caerdun. Roman occupation is proved by the remains of a settlement which when excavated revealed the outlines of a fine villa, planned in typical Roman manner with its hypocaust and rooms arranged around a large courtyard. Coins, coloured pottery and glass, and fragments of artistically decorated plaster were also found. It must have been an important settlement for it is estimated to have spread over 70 acres. From Stoke Prior a minor road soon joins up with the A44 road which soon enters Leominster.

Leominster is the second largest town in Herefordshire, and is unique in the fact that it never had its own castle, an omission that may have been responsible for the town receiving more than its fair share of strife and trouble at the hands of Welsh and English. The name of the town is of Saxon origin, and this is supported by the fact that the Mercian Earl Leofric founded a nunnery there. Leofric is less known for this than that he was the husband of the lady Godiva who stripped and *streaked* through Nottingham mounted on a white horse. A capital of a column in St Peter's Priory Church illustrates this legend, although others claim that it is a representation of Samson and the lion.

The first ecclesiastical building was a priory founded in about AD 600 by another Mercian, Merewald, who was its king. A strange story tells of Ealfred, the first abbot, feeding a ferocious lion. The fact that he was able to pacify the beast was taken as a token that the pacification of the equally fierce pagan hordes would be accomplished, and as the lion accepted food from Ealfred so would they accept conversion to Christianity.

True to form the Norman Marcher Lord De Braose sacked and burnt down the town, and next to cause suffering was Owain Glyndwr who marched through the town in 1402. Despite these unwelcome incidents the town managed to revive and prosper, becoming famous for having the finest quality wool in the Marches – much of it coming from the backs of an obscure brand of sheep known as Ryelands. A street in Hereford is called Ryeland Street.

The present Priory Church of St Peter stands on the same site where Leofric built his nunnery. For the architectural student it must be one of the most interesting in the country, for here can be traced the evolving styles of architectural development from Norman to the Perpendicular Period. In the last year of the 17th century the church was almost destroyed by fire, but six years afterwards rebuilding commenced, the last stages being completed by Sir Gilbert Scott in the late 19th century.

An interesting relic of the days when justice was summary has been preserved inside the church; this is a ducking stool which was used 'for disciplining scolds and tradesmen giving short measure'. It is recorded that it was last used in 1809 to douche two ill-tempered nags named Jenny Pipes and Sarah Secke.

The town is also rich in period architecture, perhaps the finest example being a building which, until 1853, served as a Civic Centre. When it became too small for this purpose it was carefully pulled down and re-erected in a public park. It was originally built, probably as a market hall, in 1633 by the celebrated John Abel, 'The King's Carpenter'. It is a magnificent example of a half-timbered building, its upper storey supported by arches spanning between stout wooden columns. It is now known as Grange Court, but when it served as a market hall the in-filling walls between the columns did not exist. Also erected in the park is a magnificent War Memorial designed and carved by a local man.

Two classified roads run through Herefordshire towards the northern boundary of the county. If you wish to reach Ludlow in the shortest possible time the A49 is the road to take, but if time is not important a road running parallel, the A4110, to Leintwardine will take you to several fascinating and beautiful places. The A4110 is taken just before reaching Eardisland, and after travelling a short way along it you can take a lane eastward to Kingsland. Its very name is exciting, for it suggests an ancient origin, and you will not be disappointed. A grassy mound may be all that remains of the castle built by King Merewald of Mercia, and a nearby tumulus his burial place.

Our chosen route runs through Mortimer's Cross, and the crossroads here are marked on the map with crossed swords and the date of 1461, an immediate reminder that it was here on the 2nd of February that 4,000 men died in battle on the day that 19 year old Edward Mortimer won the crown of England. An account of this important battle is contained in a previous chapter. From here you can reach Lucton, worth visiting to see the 18th century watermill which was in use up to 1940.

About two miles along the B4362 a lane on the left will bring you to Croft Castle. The first Croft is said to have built a home here before 1066, and he and his descendants played prominent parts in the history of our land. Jasper fought bravely in the Crusades, and in later years Sir Richard Croft supported the Yorkist cause at Mortimer's Cross. He survived the battle, dying about forty-eight years later, and you can see his magnificent tomb in Croft Church. Hubert Croft became Bishop of Hereford, a man of strong convictions who was never backward in expressing them. Because of this his pulpit in Hereford Cathedral nearly became his coffin when he spoke in anger to the Cromwellian troops who threatened to shoot him. Croft Castle, dating from the 14th century, is a large square quadrangular building with a circular tower at each corner. Additions were made in 1750 by Richard Knight, the ironmaster and industrialist. During the summer the castle is open to the public, who may also enjoy a walk through an impressive avenue of Spanish chestnut trees, said to have been grown from chestnuts carried by an Armada galleon which sank in the Bristol Channel. A hill above the castle once supported an even older fortification; this is known as Croft Ambrey, possibly named after the Roman Governor Aurelius Ambrosius.

Before reaching Leintwardine we pass through Aymestry and Wig-

The timbered gatehouse of Wigmore Grange, home of the abbots of Wigmore Abbey, founded by the noble Mortimers in 1179.

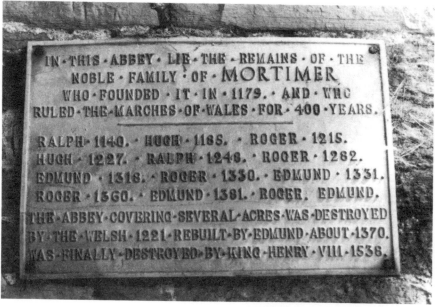

IN·THIS·ABBEY·LIE·THE·REMAINS·OF·THE
NOBLE·FAMILY·OF·MORTIMER
WHO·FOUNDED·IT·IN·1179.·AND·WHO
RULED·THE·MARCHES·OF·WALES·FOR·400·YEARS.

RALPH·1140.·HUGH·1185.·ROGER·1215.
HUGH·1227.·RALPH·1246.·ROGER·1282.
EDMUND·1318.·ROGER·1330.·EDMUND·1331.
ROGER·1360.·EDMUND·1381.·ROGER,·EDMUND,
THE·ABBEY·COVERING·SEVERAL·ACRES·WAS·DESTROYED
BY·THE·WELSH·1221·REBUILT·BY·EDMUND·ABOUT·1370.
WAS·FINALLY·DESTROYED·BY·KING·HENRY·VIII·1536.

An inscribed tablet informs the visitor that the Mortimers ruled the Marches of Wales for almost 400 years.

more. Aymestry, is at the southern end of the Lugg Valley near where the Roman Watling Street crossed the Lugg. There are traces of military activities in the trenches used by the opposing armies of the Wars of the Roses. Travellers through here in coaching days, who enjoyed watching a sporting spectacle, would have stopped at The Crown which had a cock-fighting pitch or enclosure at the rear of the inn.

Had Owain Glyndwr achieved total victory Wigmore Castle might have become a royal residence, but any plans he may have had in mind for this were frustrated when his son-in-law, Edmund Mortimer, died during the seige of Harlech Castle, and Glyndwr was forced to hide amid the mountains of North Wales. The Mortimers played a large part in history, and their castle at Wigmore was once one of the most powerful fortresses in the Marches of England and Wales. Insolent and powerful they were always quick to size up an advantageous moment, and shrewd enough to be usually on the winning side. They took every opportunity to increase their power, and were cynical enough to pacify the Welsh by inter-marriage. Gwladys, the daughter of Llywelyn the Great became the bride of a Mortimer, and in later years Edmund Mortimer found it expedient to marry one of Glyndwr's daughters.

Today there is little left to see of this Norman lair which guarded their Marcher domain, for at the end of the Civil War it was left in ruin. About two miles away near Adforton is Wigmore Grange, founded in 1179 by the Augustinians. You can still see the stonework of the gatehouse, and the building where the abbot lived. The ghost of one of the abbots is supposed to walk the ruins, searching for treasure which an earlier abbot is supposed to have hidden in the garden. Several owners have also tried to discover the treasure, defying the curse that bad luck will come to him who digs it up.

Next along our way is Leintwardine, claimed to be the Roman post of Bravonium. Aerial photographs show clear outlines of a fort laid out in the customary Roman manner. It was proved that the church stands on Roman foundations when their tiles and bricks were found under the chancel. Sheltered by hills and well watered by two rivers – the Clun and the Temme – the site would have been approved by the Romans. Just south-east is Downtown-on-the-Rock, a place also having traces of Roman occupation. Here the Temme flows between Bringewood Chase and Downton, running through a ravine where passages in the rock leading to caves may well have been fashioned by the Romans. On a ridge above the river is the 18th century pseudo castle-home of Richard Payne, a grandson of Richard Knight, a minor poet and once the member of Parliament for Ludlow. The family were 17th century ironmasters, and are said to have used wood for smelting which they cut from their estates in Staffordshire, transporting it here by mules.

West of Leintwardine at Brampton Bryan is a true Norman border castle, casting its shadow over the village which is known to be associated with the name of a famous London street. The Harleys, who gained the castle by marriage, lived here, and one of them with property in London had a street named after him. Long before this, Bryan de Brampton, builder of the 13th century castle, gave the village his name, but when the last of his line, Margaret, married Sir Robert Harley that was the end of the Brampton lineage. Sir Robert enlarged the castle, and the pride his family took in the castle was evident when one of the Harley ladies, Lady Brilliana, refused its surrender to the Royalists during the Civil War. Suffering ill health the brave lady died, so when the Royalist army took the castle they left only a gatehouse and a small portion of the main hall intact.

Above Brampton Bryan is a wooded height called Coxall Knoll which straddles the boundary between Herefordshire and Shropshire. The remains of a fortified camp gives support to the claim that it was here that Caractacus fought his last battle against the Romans, and not at Caer Caradoc north of Church Stretton in Shropshire. From Lentwardine the A4113 soon crosses the county boundary into Shropshire joining, near Bromfield, the A49 coming from Ludlow.

The direct route from Leominster to Ludlow is the A49, the distance between the two towns being 11 miles. For most of the way it runs alongside the B4361, both roads giving easy access to interesting places. North of Leominster are two houses of interest, Berrington Hall and Eye Manor. The former is also associated with the Harley family, for in 1780 it was built for the Rt. Hon. Thomas Harley. The classical Ionic columned portico gives a clue to the scale and grandeur of the mansion. Eye Manor is not as palatial as the Hall, but with well proportioned features it has an air of dignity – far more dignity than can be ascribed to its founder who, so records claim, was a Barbados slave-trader. The house was built in 1680.

Further north are Orleton and Richards Castle. Orleton is a village of charm, set around a Norman church and an old manor house. Inside the church one window has glass which has the faces of two local men, William Edwards and his son. Orleton, if the story is true that one known as Adam of Orleton conspired in the murder of Edward II, has a page in history.

Being exactly on the border of two counties the village of Richards Castle has a double claim to have a border castle, and it can also claim that it was built by a Norman noble *before* the Invasion. It was built by Richard FitzScrob who actually lived in it before the Conqueror landed at Hastings. One wonders how he was accepted by the local people who, in those times, must have treated foreigners from across the English Channel with suspicion. Except for a few fragments of stonework and suggestions of earthworks there is little to see.

Continuing north from Richard's Castle the road runs its short way through Overton to join the A49 to Ludlow, the most important town in the long and bloody history of the Welsh and English Marches.

From Builth Wells to Welshpool

Powis Castle

Welshpool

Boundary

SALOP

Kingswood

A483

Chirbury

Montgomery

A490

To Shrewsbury

Castell Dolforwyn

Churchstoke

A488

Newtown

Abermule

Balchedre Mill

A492

Kerry

Bishops Castle

Caersws

A489

Dolfor

CLUN FOREST

N

A483

B368

Cilfaesty Hill

Llanbadarn Fynydd

Beguildy

Betws-y-Crwyn Church

Clun

Dulas

A488

Beacon Hill

Llananno Church

Llanbister

Knighton

Knucklas

Abbey Cwmhir

Pilleth Site of Battle of 1401

Monaughty

Boundary

A483

Bleddfa

Presteigne

To Rhayader A44

Crossgates

RADNOR FOREST

Castell Collen

Llanbadarn Fawr Church

New Radnor

Disserth

Llandrindod Wells

Cae Du

A44

Old Radnor

A44

Kington

A483

To Hereford

To Leominster

Llanelwydd

CHAPTER TEN

From Builth Wells to Welshpool

In the last chapter our way through this borderland country of the Lords Marchers took us along routes between the present day Welsh boundary and the main A49 highway between Hereford and Ludlow – an area which the Norman invaders needed to subjugate before directing their forces to the conquest of Wales. For many centuries Ludlow was an important key-point, and a place hammered in turn by Norman and Welsh leaders. With the castles the Normans built at Hay-on-Wye, Clifford and Glasbury, and Brecon in the west to guard their rear they felt safe to march between the Epynt mountains and the Radnorshire hills through the valley of the Middle Wye to Builth, a place which became another important key-point in their plan of absolute conquest.

A route affording profitable and interesting exploration is along the A483 from Builth through Llandrindod Wells and Newtown to Welshpool, running through territory immediately west of Offa's Dyke. This area is rich in the number of prehistoric fortifications, and mounds which once bore the wood and stone strongholds of a later age – the castles of Welsh princes and of Norman barons.

The geographical position of Builth Wells, tucked between the Wye and the north-eastern slopes of Mynydd Epynt, conferred a strategical advantage, and thus provided a scene for the long years of struggle between the Welsh and the Norman invaders. It was certainly important enough for the Marcher Lord Bernard de Newmarch to persevere for thirty years to complete building a castle on the bank of the Wye. It was also important enough to receive the constant attention of the Welsh whose resentment ensured that little trace of it can be seen today.

The little market town has many memories of the past; its most sinister became perpetuated when the chief citizens refused to offer shelter to Prince Llywelyn, forcing him, according to tradition, to hide in a cold dark cave above the Wye at Aberedw. This happened in December 1282, a date which sears the pages of Welsh history for the prince was slain in a skirmish on the outskirts of Builth, and his headless corpse thrown into a roughly dug grave. This spot is now marked by an obelisk known as Cefn-y-bedd, 'The Ridge of the Grave'.

Centuries afterwards the town earned less notorious fame when it became a spa, competing with the quality, if not the taste, of its healing

The Elan Valley – 'The Lakeland of Wales'. The reservoir of Garreg Ddu.

Pastoral scene in the Elan Valley.

spring waters with Llanwrtyd Wells and Llandrindod Wells – although many visitors insist that they had received more benefit from generous libations of the Welsh cwrw, (beer) which the historian and traveller, Archdeacon Coxe described as 'new ale in a turbid state before it is clarified by fermentation, a beverage extremely forbidding to the sight and nauseous to the taste'. Today's beer is usually very different, and visitors do not come here to find a cure for an ailment by drinking spa-water, finding more interest in the beauty of the surrounding countryside, and in early summer people of all nations come to the Royal Welsh Agricultural Show held on an open meadow-land site just across the Wye at Llanelwedd.

After crossing the Wye two roads run northwards, the A470 and the A483. The former road will take you into the heart of Mid Wales, but as the purpose of this book is to encourage the reader to explore the Welsh and English Marches the A483, the one signposted to Llandrindod Wells, running through a valley between the river Ithon and the western outliers of the Radnorshire hills, is the road to take. Just before reaching Llandrindod Wells a lane on the left, after crossing the Ithon river at Disserth, will take you to Newbridge-on-Wye.

Disserth, picturesqually situated on the east bank of the Ithon is a place untouched by time, still having customs which have survived for centuries. There are records of the country games once played in the churchyard, as we discovered in the Craswall churchyard in the Black Mountains. This church also compares with Craswall, giving one a strong feeling of its antiquity, an impression heightened when seeing the primitive box-like pews, some bearing the names of the families who used them; one pew is dated 1666. Soon after the A483 passes the ancient site of the fortress of *Caer Du* we reach the outskirts of Llandrindod Wells.

In Georgian times Llandrindod was considered to be the Queen of the 'well' towns of Wales, and one which competed with the fashionable English spa city of Bath, and its chalybeate waters were said to be less distasteful but not less efficacious in quality than the springs of Builth and Llangammarch Wells. Having spacious squares and streets Llandrindod would seem to be a comparatively 'new town' its planning never restricted by a forced, but necessary, preservation of medieval foundations, and in spite of the fact that the Romans, who valued mineral waters, must have come here from their fortress of Castell Collen which is only about half a mile away.

Attempts to revive interest in spa-water have failed. One now visits the town because it is a clean pleasant place, and a convenient centre for touring. Sporting folk find its golf links and bowling greens attractive, and for the fisherman good sport can be found in the Ithon and the Wye; he can also fish in the town lake. Apart from sporting activities the town

151

provides excellent facilities for the holding of Congress meetings.

About four miles along the A438 is Crossgates, a place aptly named for roads from there run to the salient points of the compass. Going west the A44 will soon bring you to Rhayader, the starting point to reach the beautiful lake-reservoirs of the Elan Valley. The eastward branch of the A44 runs back to the Welsh border into Herefordshire.

There are several interesting ecclesiastical buildings which are easily reached from Crossgates. Just south is Llanbadarn Fawr with a church of ancient foundation whose porch contains an inscribed stone which was, for some obscure reason, brought from a nearby Roman outpost. Then about one mile north a lane leaves the A483 to follow the Clywedog stream to the ruins of Abbey Cwmhir. When the abbey was completed, towards the end of the 12th century, its nave was reputed to be longer than the nave of St David's Cathedral in Pembrokeshire. Leland confirms this fact, writing that,

> No chirche in Wales is seen of such length, as the foundation of walles there begon doth show, but the third part of the work was never finished. All the howse was despoiled and defaced by Owen Glendour.

It is claimed that the headless body of Prince Llywelyn after his death in 1282 was brought here for burial, but it has also been claimed that he was laid to rest at Cymmer Abbey near Dolgellau. The similarity of place names, and the fact that the Merioneth abbey was occupied by monks from Abbey Cwmhir, may well have caused some confusion. About five miles north-east, at the side of the A483 is Llanbister, and not far away is Llananno, places which have churches of special interest – both of them having beautiful screens and lofts. The Llananno screen, of similar workmanship to the one we saw at Llanfillo near Talgarth, is considered by many to be the finest example of Welsh woodcarving in Wales.

From Llanbister lanes run eastwards across the hills to two Welsh border villages – Knucklas and Beguildy. Knucklas, being on the border, is probably the anglicised name of Cnwclas, just as the rivers Arrow and Lugg were known to the Welsh as the Arwy and Llugwy. If you have driven over Beacon Hill the expansive views in all directions will have been appreciated. The lane from this beacon height drops down to Dulas on the B4355, and not far north from here is Beguildy. Beguildy, only just in Wales, lies in a river valley sheltered by the gentle rounded hills of Radnor. This is an area famous for its sheep, so the ancient name for the village – Beguildy, which is said to mean 'Shepherds House', is very appropriate, and even a church at Betws-y-Crwyn, on a height above Beguildy is known as the 'Church of the Fleeces'. Two rivers provide a natural irrigation, so the land is lush and green. The Teme

Llananno Church, alongside the A483 road to Newtown, has a rood screen and loft which experts consider to be the finest in the Marches of Wales.

flows close to the boundary, crossing into England just before reaching Knighton, and the River Clun, Welsh-born in the Kerry Hills, soon changes its national identity as it quickly crosses the border to carve a way through the hills to Clun. The surrounding hills are dotted with ancient stones, and there is ample evidence that the summit heights once supported the prehistoric fortifications and habitations of our ancestors.

If you have decided to take this diversion over the hills you can stay on the B4355, twisting a way along the western slopes of Kerry Hill, almost as far as Newtown. From Llanbister the A483, its northern direction dictated by the course of the Ithon, is hardly ever straight for it twists, turns and loops practically all the way to Newtown. Soon after reaching Dolfor, with the Kerry Hills behind us, the twenty-three mile journey from Crossgates to Newtown is completed.

Newtown today is a thriving agricultural centre, an industry which succeeded the days when Welsh flannel was made but it is still possible to purchase genuine Welsh weaves which, with other goods, are displayed on stalls in the High Street on the Tuesday and Saturday Market days. The High Street with several black and white timber framed buildings is impressive; most of them were wool factories, but now they have been converted into shops. The man who started the Co-operative movement in the 19th century was a native of Newtown, Robert Owen, who died soon after founding the movement but relics of this master-spinner and reformer are contained in the town's museum. Newtown seems to have seen less military action than most border towns, and the only remains of what might have been a castle of the Mortimer's are fragments in the grounds of Newtown House, yet another place which is supposed to have sheltered Charles I after Naseby. There exists a strange story that one of the Hall's owners, Sir John Pryce, was a much married man who liked to have all his wives around him – living or dead! The story is told that when he was courting his third lady she refused to marry him until he removed from his bedroom the embalmed bodies of his first two wives.

About four miles north-east of Newtown is Abermule, taking its Welsh name of Abermiwl from the Miwl stream. On a green hill above the village stood another Mortimer stronghold, but a Mortimer did not build it as this castle, known as Castell Dolforwyn, was taken by the Mortimers after the death of Prince Llywelyn. Below the ruined walls the Severn runs through a meadow which is known by the same name as the castle. Dolforwyn is said to mean 'Maiden's Meadow' so named after the legend that Sabrina, daughter of Locrine a King of England, was drowned here. Our Welsh story-teller, Geoffrey of Monmouth's account is very convincing in its detail – telling of a clandestine affair which resulted in the birth of the beautiful Sabrina. By some devious means (not made too clear by Geoffrey) Locrine's wife Gwendoline seized power and ordered her husband's bastard maiden to be thrown into a river called, according to Geoffrey, 'Habren in the British tongue, although by a corruption of speech it is called Sabrina in the other tongue'.

The A489 between Newtown and Churchstoke follows the line of the Welsh border for most of the way. Kerry is about three miles away, a place with a name associated with a brand of sheep which the Welsh claim as theirs, but Shropshire folk will contest this – so perhaps it is better to accept that they are a cross between the two, as it may also be accepted that English mutton is just as succulent as Welsh. This must have always been an area of some dispute or other, the Welsh claiming that the name of the village should be Ceri, which suggests a mountain ash, and not Kerry, finding in this a convenient excuse for rustling each others livestock. Kerry Hill is a high-point rich in historic earthworks and relics, and also a fine viewpoint for extensive vistas of a beautiful countryside. The rivers Ithon and Lugg start their journeys from these slopes to wind their way through Wales and England, but the Lugg (Llugwy) was always a Welsh river, although the Ithon too has a Welshness about its name.

Just before reaching Churchstoke the road crosses the border and breaches Offa's Dyke, and at a point midway between the new and ancient boundary a turning on the right will take you to Balchedre where, just outside the little village, you can inspect a picturesque old water-mill dating from 1747.

Churchstoke (Yr Ystog) is a turning point in our journey, for here we take the A490 and after driving three miles we reach the small town of Chirbury, a place famous for its association with the famous Herbert family. One of the most eminent members of the Herberts was Lord Edward. Unable to read at all when aged seven, at fourteen he was so skilled in languages that he went to Oxford University to continue his studies. At fifteen he married Mary Herbert who was six years older, and afterwards returned to the university accompanied by his mother and his bride.

Although a man of culture and great learning he was also a fearless soldier – his services to his country earning him a peerage. He wrote several books on philosophy and religion, his best known work being *De Veritate*. In later years Lord Edward Herbert became an agnostic, and on his death-bed he refused acceptance of the holy sacrament; in fact his comments are said to have been so offensive that the cleric refused to offer any form of spiritual comfort and absolution to the agnostical Lord of Chirbury.

Turning westwards we now go to explore Montgomery, one of the most historically important towns along our way through this land of

In the High Street and Broad Street of Newtown are many black and white timber-framed buildings. The Bear Hotel is an example.

From Montgomery Roger de Montgomery sought to control the Central Marches from a castle which the Welsh called Hen Domen. This was replaced in later years by a stone castle built by Henry III.

the Lords Marchers. Montgomery today is a town which is an almost unspoilt example of 18th century architecture. The planning is very compact with period houses and shops grouped around a large square, all presenting a Dickensian scene. The Welsh called it Trefaldwyn (Baldwin's Town) from the Norman baron Baldwin de Boller who set up a border fortress here to subjugate the Welsh. His tenancy must have been precarious for it had to be rebuilt by Henry III in 1223. Fortunes of war fluctuated in this part of the Marches from the days when Earl Roger de Montgomery was appointed by William the Conqueror to deal with Mid-Wales. The castle he built, which the Welsh called Hen Domen, rose above the border town in about 1075. Being built so soon after the Conquest, at a time when the Normans had more than enough trouble on their hands, it could not have been very substantial, and for a prolonged period of peace too near to Offa's Dyke which is only about a mile away, and still marks the boundary between Wales and England.

The Norman lair, set on a rock high above the little town, was under constant attack – the last attack being led by the redoubtable Glyndwr, but even he failed to take it. In about 1541 Sir Richard Herbert, nephew of the first Earl of Pembroke, became seneschal of the castle, and it was one of his line who surrendered the fortress to an army of Parliament led by Sir Thomas Myddleton of Chirk in 1644. This was a tame ending to a castle which had withstood so many attacks by the Welsh. Within five years the walls were torn down by the order of Cromwell. Now there is little left to see, although since 1964 the 'men from the Ministry' have been busy on works of restoration. Many interesting artefacts of medieval time, discovered during restoration, have been sent to be displayed at the Welsh Folk Museum at St Fagan's near Cardiff.

From Montgomery the B4388, joining the A483 at Kingswood, crosses the Severn river on its way to Welshpool. Just before entering Welshpool you will see on the left a large gateway and a drive which leads to the castle-home of the Earls of Powis; it stands on a gentle rise overlooking the pastures and water-meadows of the Severn Valley. The present building is of 13th to 14th century origin, but Llywelyn Fawr fought his rival Gruffydd ap Gwenwynwyn for a mound here in about 1233. The Red Castle of Powis – 'Castell Goch' was founded in 1250 by Owain ap Gruffydd, one of the Welsh opportunist princes who, to protect their own interests, were prone to inspect both sides of a fence, changing sides from Norman to Welsh. Their treacherous ways probably ensured the preservation of the castle until the Civil War; then, with many others it was 'knocked about a bit', but not too much, for Cromwell gave it to Sir Thomas Myddleton as a reward for his loyalty and help in battle. During the years following the Restoration the castle was refurbished, and now it contains some of the finest and most valuable treasures in Wales. They are all displayed in the many large

Powis Castle, near Welshpool. The gates are a fine example of the workmanship of Robert and John Davies, makers of other splendid gates for many churches and mansions in North Wales. The gates here date from 1720.

state rooms which are open to the public. The surrounding grounds are very beautiful with gardens, formal and informal, with terraced walks lined with colourful flower beds and shrubs. It is claimed that in the parkland is the tallest tree in all of Europe – a Douglas fir, 181 feet in height!

Our journey from Builth Wells through the Welsh Marches ends at Welshpool, a town which will be explored in a future chapter.

Ludlow and over Wenlock Edge to Shrewsbury

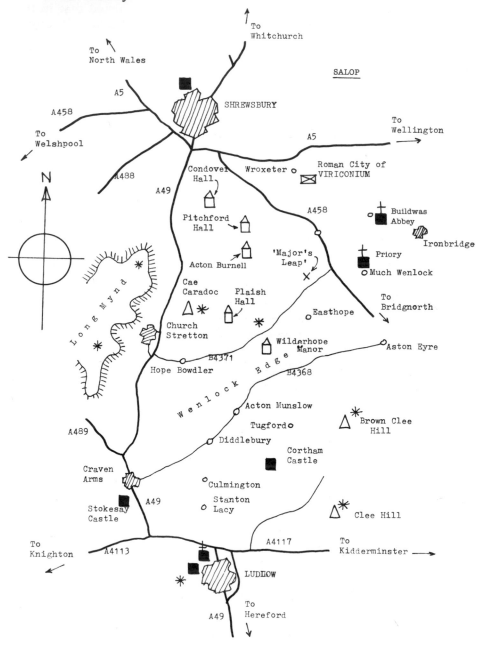

To Whitchurch

To North Wales

SALOP

A5

A458

SHREWSBURY

To Welshpool

A5

To Wellington

A488

Condover Hall

Wroxeter

Roman City of VIRICONIUM

A49

A458

Buildwas Abbey

Pitchford Hall

Ironbridge

N

Acton Burnell

'Major's Leap'

Priory

Much Wenlock

Cae Caradoc

Plaish Hall

Long Mynd

Church Stretton

Easthope

To Bridgnorth

B4371

Wilderhope Manor

Aston Eyre

Hope Bowdler

B4368

Wenlock Edge

Acton Munslow

A489

Tugford

Brown Clee Hill

Diddlebury

Craven Arms

Cortham Castle

Culmington

Stokesay Castle

A49

Stanton Lacy

Clee Hill

To Knighton

A4113

A4117

To Kidderminster

LUDLOW

A49

To Hereford

CHAPTER ELEVEN

Ludlow and over Wenlock Edge to Shrewsbury

A previous chapter described the journey from Hereford and through Leominster to the southern entrance of Ludlow. Before crossing the River Teme to enter this border town a lane on the left will bring you up to the wooded heights of Whitcliff, a viewpoint overlooking a town which has been described as 'the most distinguished looking in Britain'. A nut-shell description of Ludlow, probably viewed from Whitcliff, was given by Churchyard when he wrote,

> The towne doth stand most part upon a hill,
> Built well and fayre with streets both long and wide,
> And who that lists to walk the towne about
> Shall find therein some rae and pleasant things.

This description is still true, and old Churchyard's impressions of what he saw will be acceptable. When you look down on and over the town, its crest dominated by the high castellated tower of one of the finest parish churches in England, and the formidable grey towers and curtain walls of a large castle rising from a rock above the swift flowing Teme you will agree that few other towns have such a beautiful setting. The view from these heights is superlative. Beyond the highest part of the town are the Clee Hills, the long sharp outline of Wenlock Edge and, softened by the summer haze, the dim blue outlines of the Long Mynd and distant Wrekin.

Returning from the heights of Whitcliff we cross Ludford Bridge, a bridge which probably replaced a ford set up by the Saxons when they crossed the Teme to establish a settlement which became known as Luda. This supposition is supported by the finding of coinage of those days. Ludlow was once a walled town with seven gateways, but the only one which remains faces us as we climb up to Lower Broad Street. On the town side of the old gateway, Broad Street, flanked with cobbles and raised pavements, ascends to the Butter Market. This is a street of architectural variety, for Georgian period houses, now mostly converted into banks and offices, lining the lower end of the street soon give place to magnificent timbered buildings, the upper floors cantilevered outwards supported on ornately carved beams and brackets.

One of the most picturesque of these medieval buildings is the Angel

General view of the important border town of Ludlow from the heights of Whitcliff.

The Feathers Hotel is one of the most magnificent buildings in Luldlow.

Hotel. This was once a coaching inn, and here in 1802 Admiral Lord Nelson received honour and the title of burgess of the borough. Another fine inn, first licensed in the 16th century, is the Rose and Crown, and not far away is the well known Feathers Hotel which must surely have the finest timber-fronted facade in Britain.

It is on record that Napoleon's brother was imprisoned in a Ludlow house, and some of his belongings can be seen in the Butter Cross which now serves as the town's museum. With such strong historical interest and vast variety of architecture the charm of Ludlow is such that it is not a place through which one can hurry. Being situated in the centre of the Border country it is also a natural centre for the tourist.

Behind the Butter Cross is the large parish church of St Laurence, its beauty testifying the skill and artistry of the medieval masons and stone carvers. Early architectural styles are well represented, from the solidity of Norman design to the soaring traceried delicacy of the 15th century Perpendicular. One cannot fail to be impressed by the beauty of the glass, a beauty so exquisite that even the Despoilers of the Reformation and Civil War refrained from acts of destruction. Inspired by what they saw the glaziers of more recent years have taken care to ensure that their efforts harmonise. Representations are seen of historical figures who played such a large part in the history of the town and castle. We see figures of the Mortimers, De Clares and the De Lacys, and there are poignant motifs to remind us that the heart of young Prince Arthur, the son of Henry VII, is supposed to have been buried here – although his body was taken to rest in a tomb in Worcester Cathedral. We are also reminded by another window that two young princes, Edward and Richard, were taken from Ludlow Castle to a cruel death in the Tower of London. There are memories macabre and honourable: Saints and Devils are depicted – one saint has captured a spawn of Satan, holding him firmly by the nose with pincers. Among many fine memorials is one to the daughter of Sir Henry Sidney, Lord President of the Council of Wales. The ashes of the Shropshire poet A.E. Housman rest in this lovely church, and there are memorials to First World War heros.

In 1086 Roger de Lacy started to raise the walls and towers of the most important of the Marcher Border castles, its walls throughout the years becoming impregnated with memories of treachery and murder. For all too short a time Ludlow castle was the home of the two young sons of Edward IV who, by the order of Richard III, were taken to a mysterious death in the Tower of London. You can still see the chamber in which they once lived, and in another part of the castle is the chamber where on her bridal night Catherine of Aragon came to consummate her marriage with the inexperienced brother of Henry VIII. What actually took place that night no-one really knows, but the historian Speed claims that,

After crossing the River Teme Broad Street rises to the Gatehouse which guards the southern entry to the town of Ludlow.

A grave lady was laid between the bride and bridegroom to hinder actual consummation in regard to the Prince's green estate of body. . . . She herself applied to the censure of Henry VIII, her second husband, if he found her not a maid.

The boy prince became ill, and in the spring of 1502, within six months of his marriage with his Spanish princess he died. His body was buried in Worcester Cathedral and his heart, according to a 17th century record, was buried in the chancel of the local parish church, and at that time a memorial is said to have marked the place of burial.

In 1475 Ludlow Castle was established as the seat of the Lord President of the Marches who presided over the definitive court for the settlement of border disputes and the establishment of law and order; an arrangement which existed for about 200 years. The Royalists held the castle until July 1646, and it was the last one in Shropshire to surrender to the Parliamentarians. It continued to be used by the Council of the Marches until their rule over this borderland country was abolished in 1689. After this the castle was neglected and soon it became a ruin.

Just a short way north of Shrewsbury along the A49 trunk road a road on the right (the B4365) will bring you to Stanton Lacy a small village at the southern end of Corve Dale. Here the timber built dwellings, roofed with thatch, are clustered near a church with stonework dating its Saxon origin, but in the churchyard is stonework of more recent times, bearing the date of 1760 and inscribed with an epitaph to Thomas Davies,

Good natured, generous, bold and free,
He always was in company,
He loved his bottle and his friends,
Which brought on soon his latter end.

Our route now follows the Pye Brook north to Culmington to soon join up with the B4368 running along the southern flank of Wenlock Edge between Craven Arms and Much Wenlock, at a point marked on the map as Pedlar's Rest. The villages of Diddlesbury and Aston Munslow have some points of interest. In the churchyard of the Saxon-Norman church at Diddlesbury lies the body of Thomas Baldwin, one of the custodians of Mary Queen of Scots. He rests easier here on this Shropshire slope than when, for implication in plots on Mary's behalf, he was imprisoned in the Tower of London. His epitaph expresses his joy in escaping from,

The sea, the sword and the cruel tower.

Aston Munslow is but a small hamlet of few houses and an inn, but from here a sign directs the way to Whitehouse which has a medieval cruck-constructed hall dating back to the 14th century. An interesting feature here is that of a 'hanging staircase', similar to the one we saw at the Skirrid Inn at Llanfihangel Crucorney in Gwent. Not far away is the castle of Corfham, said to have been given to Lord de Clifford, the father of Henry II's paramour, 'Fair Rosamond', as hush money and, for obvious reasons, to retain his royal favour. A nearby well which is known as 'Rosamond's Well', may confirm this story.

Lanes through the Dale will bring you to Heath, a place from which you may climb the Clee Hills of Brown Clee, Abon Burf and Clee Burf. The latter hill supports the earthworks of a prehistoric camp. West of Brown Clee Hill is Tugford with an interesting little church containing two fertility figures called by the curious name of Sheila-na-nig's. These figures give support to the supposition that it was not unknown for pagan rites, common in this border country, to have once played a part in the ancient ceremonies held here. Indeed, there is little doubt that this area between the Clee Hills and Wenlock Edge still harbour strange memories of ancient customs and phantoms of the past. Audible phantoms, if not visual ones, are of a choir which on occasions sing at midnight at the moated Elizabethan manor of Thonglands.

At Easthope is another fine house of Elizabethan times and, for good measure, a churchyard haunted by the ghosts of two monks who during a terrible quarrel killed each other. They are supposed to rise from a mutual grave beneath a churchyard yew.

From Craven Arms, on the main A49 trunk road between Ludlow and Shrewsbury, the B4368 runs over the southern slope of the Edge towards Much Wenlock. In general Shropshire is reasonably flat, its uplands, such as Wenlock Edge, the Long Mynd and the mountains of Caer Caradoc and Wrekin rising abruptly from the lowlands. Recorded history and legend has made the most of these high places, for they all have their legends and also bear the forts and habitations of prehistoric and Romano-British man. On the northern side of the Edge, starting from Church Stretton, the B4371 also runs to the end of the Edge at Much Wenlock. About halfway along the ridge from Church Stretton a turning on the right will bring you to Wilderhope Manor, one of the best preserved Tudor-Elizabethan houses in Shropshire, and now used as a Youth Hostel. Here was once the home of the Royalist soldier Major Thomas Samwood who escaped capture by the Roundheads by jumping his horse off a nearby crag which is still called 'Major's Leap.' Another crag in this area is known as 'Ippikin's Rock' where an outlawed knight and his band of robbers were entombed in a cave after a landslide blocked the entrance. A story exists that at the right hour and time someone will speak the magic words which will clear the entrance to the cave and allow the knight and his men to come forth. Until this happens

Along Wenlock Edge is the manor of Wilderhope. It must be internationally known for it is used by youth hostellers from all parts of the world.

the knight, wearing a gold chain about his neck, is said to haunt the rock. There is a similarity to the legend that King Arthur will also appear in the entrance of his cave when the correct sequence of magical words are uttered. Such legends abound in this part of Shropshire, many of them associated with the distant Long Mynd and the serrated rock summit of the Stiperstones.

Much Wenlock is situated at the north end of Wenlock Ridge, a pleasant little town with picturesque ruins of a Priory and a half-timbered Guildhall which contains a fine collection of old furniture and several interesting relics of the past. The name of one of the saints, Ouen, who came here in 516 is preserved in a church at Rouen in France. St Ouen, whom we know as St Owen, came from Brittany to become Steward of the monastery on Bardsey Island off the coast of North Wales. His name is also perpetuated in Wenlock by the well named after him. He must have been revered by English and Welsh Christians for a street and church at Hereford, and churches in several other towns along the Welsh border have been dedicated to him.

The priory was built on the foundations of the 7th century nunnery built by St Milburga, one of the three daughters of Merewald, a high ranking noble of Herefordshire. About 200 years after it was completed it was destroyed by the Danes, despite the fact that Ethelred and his army were camped nearby. He lived up to his name of 'Unready' by taking no action to drive the Danes away. The priory was restored by Earl Leofric and Lady Godiva as a college, but soon after the Norman Conquest its walls were again torn down. In 1080, Roger de Mortimer, like other border barons wishing to ensure spiritual welfare, started to rebuild, and when his workmen discovered the tomb of the blessed St Milburga they and the monks who were to live there were overjoyed. If, after this journey along the Ridge, you are tired and thirsty, look for a nearby inn called the Robin Hood where you are welcomed by a sign which informs you that there is a new manager at the inn. It says,

Now Robin Hood is dead and gone,
Walk in and drink with Little John.

This invitation is difficult to resist.

There are other interesting ecclesiastical buildings in this area worth visiting for their beauty and historical associations. Tong church, the most interesting parish church in Shropshire, is one, a building whose architectural features compete with its ancient monuments and relics. Dr. Pevsner, in his 'Buildings of England', points this out in writing,

Tong Church is a museum of effigies to the detriment of the architecture and the individual monuments.

A feature of Wenlock Priory are the highly decorated Norman arches. The interlaced arches may have suggested the coming style of later Early English arches.

Ruins of the Cistercian abbey of Buildwas, founded in 1135 by the Bishop of Coventry and Lichfield.

There is the double tomb of Sir Thomas Stanley and his wife Margaret. The epitaph inscribed on it is said to have been composed by Shakespeare, but there is no proof of this. In the vestry are precious books, among them a Life of Christ dated 1479, and a book on English Law once owned by Queen Elizabeth I. In the vestry safe (unless it has now been removed to a safer place) is a chalice thought to have been made by Holbein in 1540. Opposite the church is a farm, but when Charles Dickens stayed there in 1838 it was an inn. You may be told that the author's Little Nell, of the *Old Curiousity Shop*, and her grandfather found solace here, and some accept it as a fact that this fictional little heroine lies buried (somewhere?) in the churchyard. As in many medieval churches, and even in some of our great cathedrals, the walls of the chancel are not in line with those of the nave, a fact supporting the theory that the chancel, representing the head of Christ inclined in anguish from his body during his awful ordeal on the Roman cross. This misalignment can be seen in so many of our churches that the statement of inaccurate setting out of the nave foundations is not acceptable.

Having come so far east of the border to see Wenlock Priory the great Cistercian abbey at Buildwas must certainly be visited. Founded in 1135 by Roger de Clinton, Bishop of Coventry and Lichfield, as a Norman abbey from time to time it must have given shelter to the enemies of the Welsh, so it is no surprise to learn that it suffered from 'the levity of the Welsh', and particularly from Glyndwr in 1406. It was built within a period of 75 years which in those troublesome times was a very short time. An unusual feature is that due to the level of the ground at the west end it lacks the usual west ceremonial entrance. The plan in the Ministry of Works booklet is somewhat vague as to where the entrance to the nave was placed. Another unusual planning arrangement (although the abbey at Tintern is similar) is that the cloister is on the *north* side of the abbey.

Readers interested in industrial archaeology will find a lot to see at three nearby places which may be regarded as 'cradles of the industrial revolution'. These places are Ironbridge, Coalbrookdale and Bewdley – although the latter place had various other industries which may be classified as craft industries.

At Ironbridge the Severn is bridged by a stupendous iron arch, the first of its kind in the world, and is a striking memorial to the recent 'Iron Age'. The ironmaster Darby cast the component parts of the great bridge here. To produce its gigantic beams the furnace must have been of mammoth proportions. Opened in 1779 the bridge took only three months to build. At Coalbrookdale the first iron steam engine cylinder was cast. A railway line was laid in 1767, and a 200 feet span bridge was erected over the Severn; Bewdley too, has a fine bridge, one which Thomas Telford designed in 1807. At Bewdley, apart from metal products, Welsh flannel and Monmouth caps were made, and there was a busy interchange of goods brought up the Severn by sailing-trows and long-boats from Bristol. After visiting the town Leland wrote,

> The towne is set on the syde of a hill, so coningly that a man cannot wish to set a towne better. At the rysynge of the sunne from the east the whole towne glittereth, being as it were of gold.

It is still a beautiful town in a lovely setting with a number of fine period houses. Earl Baldwin, three times Prime Minister of Britain was born in one of them on 3rd August 1867, and another (converted to serve as a nunnery in 1738) claims to have been the home of Prince Arthur who was married there by proxy to Catherine of Aragon. Bewdley has every reason to be proud of its long history, and also of its vanished industries.

After exploring the industrial towns along the Ironbridge gorge we return to Buildwas, and not far away from there will cross the Severn to a point where a lane is signposted to Acton Burnell. When the Domesday Book was completed this little place belonged to Roger FitzCorbet, but a century or so later its name became firmly established when it came into the ownership of William Burnell, and ultimately to Robert Burnell who became Lord Chancellor of England and also Bishop of Bath and Wells. Inside the 13th century church a brass, dated 1382, considered to be one of the finest in Britain, perpetuates the name of this illustrious family.

A short way from here are two fine Elizabethan half-timbered houses – Pitchford Hall and Plaish Hall. Built between 1560 and 1570 Pitchford Hall is considered to be the finest black and white timbered house in Shropshire. Every facade presents timber framed design in a variety of patterns, and star shaped chimneys rise high above the gabled stone-slated roofs. Memorials of the Pitchford family are in the local church, the most interesting being a huge mail-clad wooden effigy of one of the early members of the family. Later memorials span the years between 1529 to 1587; these are executed in alabaster, and show that they were a prolific family, for at the feet of their progenitors lie *fifty* children.

Plaish Hall has less happy memories, for here a story tells of a murder, and of bloodstains resulting from it that cannot be washed away. There is also a story that playing cards on a Sunday will provoke a visit from the Devil. To the north-east is Wroxeter, easily reached from Norton on the A5, but the B4380 also provides a good route.

The foundations of Wroxeter, the Roman city of Viroconium, were laid by Ostorius Scapula, the second Governor of Britain in AD 48, and from that date it was enlarged several times, assuming its greatest importance in AD 130 when the Forum was erected in honour of the

At Ironbridge the River Severn is spanned by a striking memorial to the recent 'Iron Age'.

The impressive ruins of the Roman city of Viroconium *near Wroxeter.*

Emperor Hadrian. From its inception building work must have constantly been interrupted by the local tribes, but in time, as the Silurians occupied the Roman town of Caerwent in Gwent, it became a settlement for the Cornovii tribe. This probably happened after the Roman garrison (the VIV) moved to a new base in Chester about AD 88. The city walls are said to have enclosed an area larger than Pompeii, containing civil buildings, baths, temples and a magnificent Forum. After the Romans left this country to defend their falling Empire the once proud city became a ruin, so when the Saxons arrived they found its broken streets and walls a desolate and uninviting place.

It was in an even worse condition when the Norman invaders saw it, but they used the ruined city as a quarry to provide them with ready cut stone for building their castles and churches. It was regarded as an evil haunted place and until about 1702, when a tessallated pavement was uncovered, it was left alone. Stories of buried treasures prompted further excavations to be carried out, and part of the 400 feet frontage of the Forum and other buildings were uncovered. Apart from relics of Roman times the only treasure found, clutched in the skeleton hand of a man, was a number of Roman coins. Near the man there was also found the skeletons of two women and that of a slaughtered child whose body had been thrown over a courtyard wall. Many relics are displayed in a museum on site, and others can be seen in Shrewsbury Museum. One of the most interesting displays on the wall of the site museum is part of a stone which had been set in a wall of the Forum. It has been translated to read,

TO THE EMPEROR CAESAR TRAJANUS HADRIANUS AUGUS-
TUS, SON OF THE DEIFIED TRAJANUS PARTHICUS, GRAND-
SON OF THE DEIFIED NERVA, PONTIFEX MAXIMUS, CONSUL
FOR THE THIRD TIME, FATHER OF HIS COUNTRY, THE COM-
MUNITY OF THE CORNOVII ERECTED THIS BUILDING.

After the Romans left Britain, unable to defend this Romano-British city from the Saxons, the soft living citizens moved to a site encircled by a loop of the Severn. They built there a new town which they called Pengwen, renamed later by the Saxons as Scrbbesbyrig, 'Shrub-town', which we now know as Shrewsbury, a town just five miles away which we shall explore later.

Stokesay Castle, Shropshire Hills and Shrewsbury

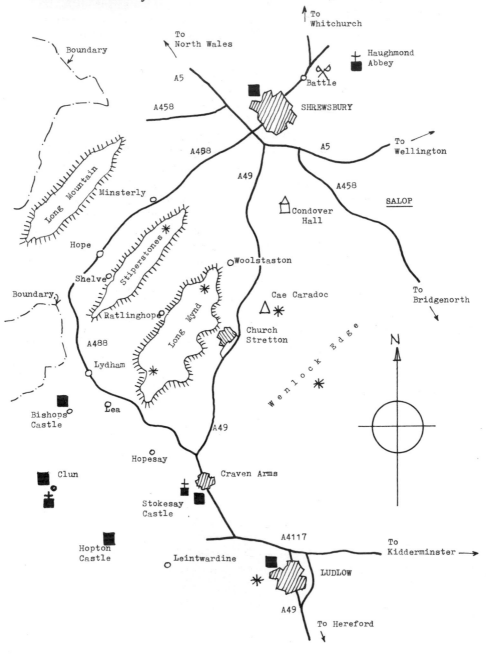

CHAPTER 12

Stokesay Castle, Shropshire Hills and Shrewsbury

Just before reaching Craven Arms the towers of a church and castle are seen, and a sign on the left indicates the way to Stokesay Castle, recognised as being one of the finest examples of a fortified manor house in England, its first stones being laid about the middle of the 13th century. Within 50 years it was a residence grand enough to offer shelter and entertainment to the highest in the land. One of its finest features is the Great Hall, more than 50 feet long and covered with a high roof supported by massive 'crucks' braced by equally large collar-beams.

When the Norman Lacys held the land here after the Conquest the fortress they built would, for safety, require surrounding by a moat; the line of this moat is still traceable. Times had improved by 1281 when Lawrence, a rich wool merchant, bought the castle so he added a solar and the present spacious Hall, additions which were considered elegant and comfortable enough to impress and entertain a Bishop of Hereford. During the Civil War it was a Royalist outpost supporting Ludlow Castle, but happily it was never seriously attacked, so when it surrendered it was not 'slighted'. Space does not permit a detailed description which this interesting building deserves, but an excellent guide book can be obtained from the gatehouse custodian.

Just beyond the castle is Craven Arms, a place which is said to have taken its name from a coaching inn. Today it serves as a signpost on the main highway to Shrewsbury, but in the autumn it comes alive, for thousands of sheep are brought or driven here from the surrounding countryside for sale.

From Craven Arms the B4368, after crossing the line of the ancient Watling Street of the Romans on its way between Leintwardine (Bravonium) to Wroxeter (Viroconium) runs in a westerly direction to Clun. The low hills on the north side of the road are dotted with prehistoric camps, and just after crossing the Roman road a lane will take you along the wooded slopes of Hopesay Hill which is a delectable National Trust Area. Below the hill, standing in 'God's Acre', is a late 13th century church and the ruins of a castle. The B4368 follows the River Clun, and about halfway between Craven Arms and Clun a minor road crosses the river to run through a shallow valley to Hopton Castle, one given by Henry II to one of his supporters in 1165. The very sight of this square

The tower of Clun church, as strong and solid as a Norman keep.

keep must have enraged the Welsh, but the 10 feet thick walls were strong enough to withstand and abort any attack. If any Marcher border fortress is haunted this grim ruined Norman castle must surely be, for in 1644, after resisting for three weeks, its mound became slippery with the blood spilling from the thirty-three Roundheads who, after surrender, were massacred by Royalist soldiers.

Clun takes its name from the river which has a picturesque saddleback bridge. The small village lies on both sides of the bridge, so the old saying that 'those who crossed the bridge came back sharp' becomes inapplicable. Whether they were chased back *sharply* by the Welsh, or if they returned more astute is not certain. Casting a black shadow over the village are the grey stone walls of yet another border castle. Fought over by two nations Clun was never wholly English or Welsh, and its name, as other place-names in this area, is of Celtic origin. Prince Llywelyn attacked the castle in 1195, and Owain Glyndwr followed suit in later years, but it was finally made a ruin during the Civil War.

The tower of the church, built like a Norman keep, suggests that Clun was often the scene of much fighting, so would have often changed hands as it was occupied in turn by Welsh and English. This is a fact borne out by the churchyard tombstones inscribed with such Welsh names as Cadwalladr, Meredith, Hughes and Pugh.

When Sir Walter Scott, who had relatives in this area, was searching for a suitable locale and castle to fit his description of the *Garde Dolareuse*, in his novel *Betrothed*, it is suggested that he found it here. Proof that he stayed here is recorded in the visitors book of the Buffalo Inn.

Not far along the A488, which will eventually bring us to Shrewsbury, is Bishop's Castle. Mary Webb, another author seeking local interest and colour, described Bishop's Castle and other Shropshire towns and villages in her book *Mallard's Keep*. There is little to be seen of the castle, and if the keep once stood on a mound this has now been flattened to form a bowling green. The Bishops of Hereford held tenure here, but there is more to remind us of them about two miles away at Lea where one of their possessions – a massive keep – adjoins a 16th century farmhouse.

A lane from Lea brings us back to the main road where we turn left for Lydham, a place also having a strong squat keep-like Norman church tower. The A488, after skirting the south-west flank of the Stiperstone Hills enters the Hope Valley. On the western side of the Stiperstones is Shelve where the Romans mined for lead; this being confirmed by the finding of lead pigs stamped with the name of Hadrian (AD 117–38) Roman tools, coins and pottery were also found. There are still traces of stone buildings used by the miners who worked here up to the middle of the 19th century, but their overgrown waste heaps now blend with the landscape. A short way further north the small hamlet of Hope also

Stokesay Castle – the Gatehouse.

has abandoned heaps of waste tips and skeletal buildings which remind us of an industrial past.

Next comes Minsterley, about halfway between Lydham and Shrewsbury, and at the end of the Hope Valley. Here was the setting used by Mary Webb for her Shropshire novel *Gone to Earth*. Mary was born at Leighton on 25th March 1881, and died at the early age of 46. She is buried at Shrewsbury.

Before reaching Shrewsbury two ranges of hills lying east of Minsterly invite exploration. It is possible to reach this hill country from Minsterly but the narrow lanes to these heights are steep and very devious, so it is better to return to the A49 trunk road just north of Craven Arms and drive on to Church Stretton.

Church Stretton, lying between the Long Mynd (Long Mountain) and the Caradog ranges, always appears to be a busy bustling little town, its streets and squares usually filled with cars. Years ago when fairs were held there the one held just before Christmas had the uninviting title of 'Deadman's Fair'. It was called this because so many who struggled homewards across the Shropshire hills, particularly the Long Mynd, often perished. A story of 1865 tells of how the Rev. Donald Carr, after he had conducted service in a nearby valley church, took nearly 24 hours to fight his way home through a severe blizzard on the Long Mynd.

Burway Hill, starting from the west end of the town, ascends the flank of the Long Mynd. It is a steep and narrow track running up a ledge cut in the mountain above the Cardingmill Valley, a popular place with summer visitors. A favourite walk from this valley is up to the Light Spout Waterfall and to the Devil's Mouth.

The Long Mynd is a natural barrier between England and Wales, a whale-back ridge criss-crossed with ancient tracks. As you ascend the narrow track above the deep Cardingmill Valley the British camp of Brodbury comes into view, and if before reaching the highest point of this single track road you can find room to park the car in a layby there is a magnificent view back over Church Stretton. Wenlock Edge gradually rises from the low-lying valley floor, and also the mountains of Caer Caradog and Wrekin. Before the ancients built a ditch and rampart fort on the Wrekin's summit the mountain was considered volcanic, throwing 'fires of lower earth to sky'. It is also said to be the oldest hill in England, and must have been if it was formed in the days when the Devil was abroad, for here, so the legend claims, he created a mound to dam the Severn for the purpose of drowning the people of Shrewsbury. Folk now living there would be inclined to give credence to this legend. The extensive earthworks on the summit are remains of an ancient camp, one which may have been occupied by the Cornovii tribe before they found better accommodation at Wroxeter.

When the top of the Long Mynd is reached a drive southwards along

13th-century Stokesay Castle is one of the finest examples of a fortified manor house along the Welsh border.

Stokesay Castle was a Royalist outpost supporting Ludlow Castle, but it was never seriously attacked.

the old Port Way will bring the Welsh mountains into view, an impressive backcloth over a patchwork of green fields. After rain a clear atmosphere will unveil the distinctive outlines of Cader Idris, the Arans, and the less recognisable shapes of the Berwyns and Plynlimon.

At certain times, if one is at all sensitive, a journey across the Long Mynd can be atmospheric; there is a strange and timeless feeling that one is travelling away from the present and the future into the past. There are deep cwms and hollows with cloud-shadowed pools, all haunted by the ghosts of those who perished on the Mynd. On a day when mists swirl and obscure the way ahead it is easy to imagine that Wild Eric and his Saxon warriors will suddenly appear; Eric sounding an eerie call on his battle-horn to signal the Welsh to ride down the mountain with him and drive away the Norman invaders. All this is not so fanciful as it may sound, for a legend avers that Eric appears when war is about to break out, and his last *recorded* appearance was just before the Battle of Waterloo. A less fearsome apparition is that of the White Lady who has been known to join in local dances. Eric, a Saxon Earl of Shropshire, loved to fight, and he was quite impartial. He fought with the Welsh against the Normans, and with the Normans he fought the Scots.

Across miles of open country are seen other Shropshire hills – the Stiperstones and the Long Mountain near Welshpool. The Stiperstones, recognised by a ridge 'of jagged rocks like a prehistoric monster', is also claimed to be haunted by Wild Eric, and fey local folk have many strange tales to tell of him. A cluster of rocks on the ridge resemble a large chair, said to have been formed when Satan overloaded his apron with stones and the strings broke so that the stones fell into the shape of a chair. True or not, the 'Devil's Chair' is visible for miles around. Some say that it was here that Caractacus fought his last battle against the Romans, but others insist that it was on the lower slopes of the hill near Church Stretton which bears his name, and another site in Herefordshire claims the honour for the same reason. Most of these claims are based on the description of the scene of his last battle as written by a contemporary roman historian; each site complying with the historical account.

Mary Webb made good use of the Shropshire landscape and hills, particularly in her earliest novel *The Golden Arrow*. The Stiperstones became the *Diafol Mountain*, a name with a Satanic connotation. *Gone to Earth*, is set in this area, and her *Black Huntsman* must surely have been inspired by Wild Eric.

With a good map, a good sense of direction, or, better still, a good guide, one can find a safe way down from the Mynd to reach Ratling-hope, turning there to reach Woolstaston, a charming village with timbered houses fronting a green. In less than ten minutes the main road at Leebotwood is reached where The Pound Inn, which first served

View of the Shropshire Hills and Cardingmill Valley from the Lond Mynd.

One of the most interesting coffeehouses in Shrewsbury, adjoining the church-yard of St. Alkmund.

ale in 1650, was a welcome halt in the days of cattle-droving. On the way to Shrewsbury a signpost directs the way to Condover where the Hall, surrounded by well kept gardens, must be one of the largest and finest Elizabethan period houses in Shropshire.

In 1483, at the small hamlet of Glyn, Old Parr, the Methuselah of Shropshire was born. He lived to a ripe old age, being almost 153 when he died in 1635. Born during the reign of Edward IV he lived a full life during the reign of ten English kings and queens. At the age of 105 he seduced young Catherine Milton who bore his child; for this he was ordered to make public atonement clad in nothing but a thin shirt inside Allerbury church. Hearing of the astounding career and liveliness of the aged Shropshire rustic the Earl of Arundel took him to London. After being presented to Charles I he was feted and lavishly entertained, but not being used to the rich fare and excitement of the London way of life he died on the 13th November 1635. A brass plate in the church tells us that,

> The Old, very Old Man Thomas Parr. Was born at Glyn in the year of Our Lord 1483. He lived in the reign of ten Kings and Queens of England; Edward IV., Edward V., Richard III., Henry VII., and VIII., Edward VI., Queen Mary, and Queen Elizabeth, James I, and Charles I. Died on the 13th November 1635 and was buried in Westminster Abbey . . . aged 152 years and 9 months.

Thomas certainly lived and enjoyed life to the full!

Another notable Shropshire character was 18th century John Mytton, the squire of Halston. Due to his wild way of living he did not live as long as old Parr, for he died aged 37. A typical Regency Rake, he led a spectacular life drinking, womanising and ready to place a wager on anything. He rode hard and drank hard, always eager to attempt some audacious deed with complete contempt for danger. One day, suffering from hiccoughs, he set fire to his night-shirt to effect a cure. It was fortunate that two friends were at hand to quench the flames. His exploits caused him to be known as 'Mad Jack Mytton', and brought him to a period of mental derangement. Eventually arrested for debt he was locked up in Shrewsbury jail. Despite his wildness people thought well of him, for when he died 3,000 people attended his funeral, and shutters covered the windows of Shrewsbury shops when the funeral cortege passed through the town.

Shrewsbury is known to many as the 'Town of Flowers', a title appreciated by all who visit in August when the town is bedecked in flowers and the annual Floral and Musical Festival is held in the local park. The early name of the town must have confused the map-makers. It was once called Caer Amwyithig, 'the Town of the Shrubs', but when the Saxons fought their way across the Severn they called it Scrobbes-byrig, 'the Burgh of the Shrubs'. Leland, a keen observer of topography, wrote that,

> The towne of Shrobbesbyri
> Standeth on a rokky hill of stone
> Of a sadde redd earth, and Severne
> So girdethe in all the towne that
> Saving a little pece . . . it were an isle.

As the town is almost enclosed in a loop of the Severn Leland's description is apt, the riverside settlement probably came into existance when the Cornovii tribe settled here after the Roman Viroconium (Wroxeter) was destroyed about 150 years after the Romans left Britain. King Offa of Mercia evidently favoured the settlement, and naming it Sloppesbury he made sure that it was well on the east side of his dyke.

The town really began to expand during the years following the Conquest when Roger de Montgomery set up his motte within a loop of the Severn. News of this brought the Welsh, in 1069, storming across the dyke, and aided by Eric the Wild, who enjoyed being in the thick of battle, they entered the bailey, tore down the Norman's palisade and set fire to the town. A stone castle was not built until the reign of Henry II. As well as building a more durable castle the Normans replaced many of the existing primitive Saxon churches with ones built of stone. To secure the town they surrounded it with walls, so with the river on three sides it was almost impregnable, and it also served as a base for expeditions against the Welsh.

Led by Llywelyn Fawr the town was captured in 1215 by the Welsh who managed to hold it until driven out by Edward I. It was Edward, 'the Castle Builder', who improved the defences, encircling that part of the town not facing the Severn with stout walls and guardhouses. About 200 years later Owain Glyndwr laid siege, but his forces retired when the English, led by Prince Hal of Monmouth, drove them away. From the middle of the 13th century, despite attacks from the Welsh the town became established, and in the 14th century it was an important centre of the wool trade. This was a period when many of its finest houses and churches were built. War gave place to trading, inspiring Defoe to write,

> They all speak English in the town, but on Market Day you would think you were in Wales.

A view over the town from a height – possibly from the top of one of the multi-storey car parks – will substantiate the claim that here is 'England's finest Tudor town', and a walk through the streets will allow closer examination and appreciation of its medieval splendour. Most of the many black and white timbered houses are now used as shops, banks and hotels, but the ancient inns still retain their original identity. At one of the inns Paganini played his 'Devil's fiddle', and at the Lion Hotel Jenny Lind, 'the Swedish Nightingale' sang. Near this inn is a house which lodged Henry Tudor on his way to win the English crown at Bosworth.

The town has more than thirty churches, these and certain schools evoke memories of the past. Two of the oldest churches are St Alkumund's founded in 911 by Ethelbleda, daughter of Alfred the Great, and St Mary's which was founded in the same century. In 1793 the latter church was the scene of a daring feat which ended in tragedy. This happened when a man named Cadman strung a rope from the 200 feet high spire across the Severn, using it, so he hoped, to provide a quick and spectacular descent. His slide from the top of the spire had hardly commenced when the rope snapped and he fell to his death. A plaque on an external wall of the church recalls the event.

Shrewsbury School is built on the site of a cross where Dafydd, brother of Llywelyn the Last was cruelly executed in 1283, and in later years Hotspur was hanged drawn and quartered. The school, founded in 1551, had many famous scholars; among them were Sir Philip Sydney (1554–1586), and Charles Darwin (1809–1882), who was a native of Shrewsbury.

The oldest part of the town is of a similar character to York. In Grope Lane, which runs as a narrow alley between High Street and Fish Street, the upper stories of the buildings overhang and almost meet over the paved way between. This is an economical method of medieval planning hard to equal. At the top of the alley covered steps, known as Bear Steps, lead up to a courtyard in front of St Alkumund's church. Adjoining the steps are two timber-built buildings dating from about 1440; they are particularly well preserved and truly representative of the town's antiquity.

Two places closely connected with the history of Shrewsbury and the Marches should now be visited; these are Battlefield and Haughmond Abbey. Battlefield is just north of Shrewsbury and is the scene of the battle of 1403 when Henry IV defeated Hotspur, although Shakespeare credits his boastful knight Falstaff for putting an end to Hotspur's aspirations. Falstaff boasted that he slew his formidable adversary in single combat after fighting 'a long hour by Shrew' clock'. As an act of thanksgiving and to commemorate the Battle of Shrewsbury the king founded a church. As a tribute to his memory and generosity a statue of him in his battle-armour stands in a niche inside the church.

Our journey ends at Haughmond Abbey, a picturesque ruin alongside the A5062, a short way east of Shrewsbury. The building dates from

Grope Lane, Shrewsbury. A narrow passageway linking the High Street with Fish Street.

1135 and, as usual, the Cistercians chose an ideal site on which to build where the soil was rich and wood was plentiful. As they were an inconvenient distance away from a river they saw to it that the fishponds they constructed would always provide an ample supply of their favourite food.

Welshpool to Prestatyn

CHESHIRE

Dee Estuary

Prestatyn Dyserth

To Abergele

Rhuddlan

A5151

Caerwys
R. Fort

A55

Boundary

St. Asaph

Bodfari

R.Dee

To Chester

Denbigh

R. Clwyd

N

Mold

CLWYD

A525

Ruthin

A494

Castell-y-Rhodwydd

'Worlds End'

Horseshoe Pass

Valle Crucis

A483

A494

Dinas Bran

To Betws-y-Coed

A5

R.Dee

Berwyn Mountains

Corwen

Glyndyfrdwy

Chirk

To Whitchurch

Llangollen

Llanarmon Dyffryn Ceiriog

Glyn Ceiriog

Tan-y-Pistyll Waterfall

Gobowen

Llansilin

A495

Llangynog

Sycharth

Oswestry

Llanrhaeadr-ym-Mochnant

Lake Vyrnwy

Penybontfawr

Llynclys

A5

Llanwddyn

Llanfyllin

A483

To Shrewsbury

Treladyn Hall

Boundary

A490

A458

A458

Powis Cas.

Welshpool

SALOP

CHAPTER THIRTEEN

Welshpool to Prestatyn

Although close to Offa's Dyke and the present boundary between Wales and England Welshpool escaped much of the conflict and suffering endured by many other towns in the Marches. No records exist that the motte and bailey on the east side of the town was ever seriously threatened. Any conflict disturbing the peace here must have taken place around the Red Castle about a mile to the south, although in August 1644 a street battle was fought between the Royalists and Roundheads who afterwards marched off to capture Powis Castle. An echo of Civil War fighting can be found on the door of a house where nails are arranged to read 'God damn old Oliver, 1661'.

An inscription on a corner house in the High Street dates the origin of it as 1692 when it was the home of Gilbert and Ann, descendants of Robert Jones, reputed to be the first Welsh *Jones*. Grace Evans was born in a house near the church, a brave woman who helped a daughter of Lord Powis free her husband from the Tower of London in 1716. The prisoner walked out, dressed as a female, as his wife's servant.

The parish church is not as interesting as some of the relics it contains. One, which present day druids might take exception to, is Maen Llog, thought to have been an ancient altar stone, and later used as a throne for the Abbot of Strata Marcella, a Cistercian abbey whose ruins are about three miles away. Perhaps the greatest of Welshpool's treasures is an Early Iron Age Celtic shield which can be seen in the town museum.

In the 13th century Welshpool was a Chartered market town, famous for cattle, sheep, wool and Welsh flannel. Goods were brought along the Severn by sailing trows and in later years by canal and train. Restoration of the canal is in hand and stretches of it can by explored by dinghies and small powered boats. Railway enthusiasts can ride through delightful countryside from a Halt on the western side of the town to Llanfair Caereinion; these excursions run from Easter to early October.

One of the finest black and white timbered houses in Wales can be seen a few miles north of Welshpool. Built on the site of a recorded Roman villa named 'LATEO' Trelydan Hall dates back to the 15th century. It is now a Guest House, its owners inviting visitors to enjoy home-made traditional Welsh dishes, and in the Great Hall, warmed by

Some of the old houses of Welshpool have been converted into shops and restaurants.

Trelydan Hall, one of the finest houses in the Marches, is claimed to stand on the site of a Roman villa.

giant log fires, they can listen to Welsh harpists and singers, and also see Welsh clog dancing at its best.

Welshpool is a good centre for exploration of the borderlands and the Berwyn Mountains. The A490, soon after crossing the River Vyrnwy, reaches Llanfyllin, a starting point for a visit to the beautiful mountain-enclosed Lake Vyrnwy. Years ago Llanfyllin was noted for its fine ale, a potent brew if the old saying that 'old ale fills Llanfyllin with young widows' is true, so perhaps it is as well that this strong Welsh *cwru* (beer) is no longer fermented there. Charles I is said to have received a welcome and a warm bed here, and the bed-warmer he used was prized by his host who was known as Price the Papist. It is also claimed that the king left an even more tangible reminder of his stay, for about 100 years ago a family claimed direct descent from his bastard child. Visitors here are usually on their way to Llanrhaeadr-ym-Mochnant from where a wooded valley leads to Tan-y-pystyll and a waterfall which is one of 'the Seven Wonders of Wales'. George Borrow wrote of it,

> I never saw water falling so gracefully, so much like thin beautiful threads as here.

The beautiful fall pours a cascade of white water, falling from the Berwyn Moors some 250 feet above a wooded cwm. After falling into a bowl in the rock it spews out a second cascade through a hole in the side of the rocky cauldron.

Llanrhaeadr-ym-Mochnant was known as the home of the Rev. William Morgan (1540–1604) who translated the Bible into Welsh. It was published in 1588, and as by then William had become the Bishop of St Asaph it became known as 'the Bishop's Bible'. The church in which William Morgan preached is one which gives the village its name and means 'the church by the falls of the brook of the pigs'. There may be slightly different versions of translation, but this one is good enough to be an example of the Welsh way of inventing descriptive place-names.

Just south of the village, near a school, is an ancient standing stone now called 'Post Green', bearing the inscription VIATORVIA SOLATIO ET COMMODITATI, 'For the comfort and convenience of wayfarers', and also A SALOP XXVI, A LOND CLXXX. It is thought that the inscriptions were done in 1770 as ordered by the vicar of that time. Not very far away, near a tumulus, is another standing stone at a spot known as Post-y-Wiber, 'the post of the Winged Serpent'. Old stories tell of the havoc wrought in this neighbourhood by a fearsome winged beast, who devoured sheep, cattle, and humans, finding young children particularly tasty morsels. Plans to get rid of the voracious creature were many, but not successful until someone wise in the way of slaying dragons laid a trap. A large pillar was set up, and this was studded with

From the lowlands beyond Welshpool the mountain road climbs to negotiate the Milltir Gerrig Pass to Bala. View of the valley below.

The vast expanse of the Berwyn moors which has been called 'the Roof of Wales'.

spikes which were concealed under a cloak of red material. When the dragon saw this he was incensed, and after attacking the stone for several hours he died from exhaustion and loss of blood.

Following the River Tanant the B4396 passes close to the large mound of Bryn Dinas, an ancient earthwork rising 900 feet above the Tanant Valley. When the Green Inn at Llangedwyn is reached a turning on the left turns north to Llansilin. About halfway between the Green Inn and Llansilin is a mound beside the River Cynlleth which marks the site of Sycharth, one of Glyndwr's castle-homes. Llansilin is a pleasant little village with a 13th century church with features which remind us of the part the building played during the Civil War. The fact that the church was fortified then is evident by the bullet holes left by Civil War muskets. In the churchyard is the tomb of the Royalist Huw Morris, a soldier and poet, who died in 1709.

The surrounding hills bear evidence of occupation and activities of times before the Romans and Normans brought their armies across the border. Ancient tracks are overlaid by Roman roads, the one most favoured by the map-makers, is the Sarn Helen which can be traced from South to North Wales. Helen was a beautiful native princess who, according to legend and the Mabinogion, married the Roman General Magnus Maximus. Helen is said to have accompanied her Roman husband on most of his expeditions, and a story in the Mabinogion claims that she was responsible for making his journeys easier. The Mabinogion, compiled from fascinating Celtic legends, tells us that,

> Helen bethought her to make high roads from one castle to another throughout the island of Britain. And the roads were made. And for this cause they are called the roads of Helen Luddawe, that she was sprung from a native of this island, and the men of the Island of Britain would not have made these great roads for any save her.

Few hills in this area fail to reveal the shafts and workings of the Romans who laboured, with conscripted workers, to enrich the coffers of their homeland by the extraction of silver, lead and copper. In 1761 a cave called 'Ogo's Hole' revealed a rich find of Roman coins, and in 1965 a further hoard was unearthed by some local lads. These finds, ruled to be 'Treasure Trove' are now displayed in the museum at Oswestry. Just across the border, where the River Tanant is a favourite one with anglers, is Llan-y-Blodwell, a village with some delightful cottages and a 14th century inn, is as pretty as its name suggests – which may be translated as the village, or enclosure, of the flowers.

On reaching Llynclys the A483 will bring us to Oswestry, a town which derives its name from that of the Northumbrian King Oswald who was defeated in battle by Penda, King of Mercia. Being a pagan who detested Christians Penda crucified Oswald, nailing his mutilated body to a tree. This happened in 642, and not long afterwards Oswald was made a saint and a well, reputed to cure blindness, was named after him. At this time it is probable that the people occupied the Iron Age camp to the north; a reasonable supposition as it is known as Old Oswestry. The present town, remembering the circumstances of Oswald's death was called 'Oswald's Tree'.

Soon after the Conquest the Norman FitzAlan was appointed to create a lordship here to hold down the Welsh. That he failed to do so is evident by the fact that little can be seen of the castle or the town walls. The town was attacked by English and Welsh – being burnt down by King John, then by Llywelyn Fawr in 1223, and almost 200 years later by Owain Glyndwr. Not only war ravaged the town for in 1559 a plague decimated the population. An ancient stone, part of a cross, known as the Croeswylan Stone, 'the Cross of Weeping', reminds one of this sad event.

At the end of the First World War a large prisoners' camp was converted into an Orthopaedic Hospital. Known as the Agnes Hunt and Robert Jones Hospital it has an international reputation. Two other people brought fame – the poet Wilfred Owen who was killed in the First World War, and the composer Sir Henry Walford Davies who did so much to promote appreciation of classical music.

Chirk brings us back into Wales again. The Welsh called it Y Waun, a name linked with the great castle on a hill to the west of the town called Castell y Waun, 'the Castle in the Meadow'. Built in the 13th century it became one of the most important Marcher strongholds along the borders of Wales, and remained so until it became the home of the Myddletons in the 16th century. The present castle was largely built by Roger Mortimer on land which his king had given him for helping to suppress the Welsh and putting an end to the aspirations of Llywelyn, the last native Prince of Wales. When Mortimer held the castle a casual visitor would have been held and questioned long before reaching the entrance, but nowadays visitors are welcomed.

When a site was chosen it was no doubt considered that Offa's Dyke, which almost touches the castle walls, would be a barrier to deter attack from the west, but hundreds of Welsh and English dead were buried here after the fierce battle between Henry II and Owain Gwynedd, the Prince of North Wales. During the battle Hubert de Clare met his death shielding the body of his royal master from a Welsh arrow. In later years the surrounding hills echoed from the sound of Civil War cannons. Since then it has been converted into a comfortable residence. The archers' loop-holes, designed for defence, have been replaced with large mullioned windows which look completely out of place. The elegance of Tudor, Elizabethan and other days can be seen everywhere, the richly appointed rooms containing exquisite period furniture and many fine works of art. One room has a four-poster bed used by Charles I, and his rival Cromwell left a pair of jackboots to remind us of his stay. The entrance gates to the castle grounds are especially distinctive, the work of two brothers Robert and John Davies who made other fine gates for mansions and castles in this part of Wales.

From Chirk a road follows the River Ceiriog into the Ceiriog Valley, a delectable unspoilt stretch of Welsh countryside watered by clear trout filled streams. Years ago a tramway ran through the valley bringing slate and quarried stone from the hills to Chirk. If you are interested in the industrial activities of the past a road will bring you to the caverns of the Chwarel Wynne mine and museum. Some of the old workings have been restored and there are guided tours through the vast underground workings. You may also examine the tools and equipment used to cut and process the slate. Here and there are craft centres with workshops where pottery and hand made furniture is still made. There are centuries old inns; one, The Swan, which dates back to the 13th century, sells ale which met with the approval of George Borrow.

John Ceiriog Hughes, (Ceiriog) poet and librettist, was born in this beautiful valley in 1832. He is known as the composer of 'God Bless the Prince of Wales'. Thomas Jefferson, (1743–1826) a President of the United States of America was a close relative of folk who lived in this part of the Welsh borderland.

When Glyn Ceiriog is reached the valley road bends southwards to Llanarmon Dyffryn Ceiriog, a charming little village tucked neatly in between two of the Berwyn spurs. From here lanes run over the moors in all directions; one leads to a scenic waterfall, but a student of Welsh history will know that he is in 'Glyndwr territory' for if other lanes are followed they will bring him to two of the old warrior's favourite homes. One is at Glyndyfrdwy near Corwen, but tracks across the mountains must be taken to reach it. The other, burnt to the ground by Prince Hal of Monmouth in 1403, was at Sycharth, a castle according to the bard Iolo Goch, which stood,

Upon four wooden columns proud
Mounteth his mansion to the cloud.

Iolo's poem 'Sycharth' suggests that it was a wooden castle, but all that can be seen today is the mound on which it stood, and a vague suggestion of the moat and some shallow hollows which may have been fishponds.

Just beyond Chirk the Vale of Ceiriog is bridged by Telford's famous aqueduct carrying the Shropshire Union Canal towards Llangollen where another of the clever engineer's aqueducts crosses the River Dee.

The River Dee at Llangollen, a favourite place of visitors and tourists to North Wales.

The abbey of Valle Crucis, one of the reputed burial places of Owain Glyndwr. Onetime religious centre and burial place of Welsh nobles and princes.

Both are most impressive, the latter supported by 14 arches is 120 feet above the river, and at 1,000 feet is the longest aqueduct in Britain.

A short way north of Chirk a 'Y' road junction is reached, the A5 turning west to Llangollen and the A48 northwards to cross the Welsh border at Pulford on its way to Chester. As the end of this part of our journey through the Welsh Marches is intended to end near Prestatyn the A5 is taken to Llangollen.

Llangollen, a favourite place with tourists in Wales, became widely known from 1947 when its Midsummer Festival of music and dancing became an international event. The beauty of this Dee-side town and its setting can best be appreciated if, before crossing the river bridge, you take a narrow lane to the top of a hill overlooking the town and valley. This viewpoint is marked on Bartholomew's map No. 23 with a red star. From this spot on the northern escarpment of the Berwyns there is a wide panoramic view; to the west road and river run a twisting course between the Berwyn and the Llantysilio Mountains; in the north another valley route runs between the Llantysilio and Eglwyseg Mountains where the ruins of Dinas Bran, 'Crow City', stand on a cone shaped knoll high above Llangollen.

Madog ap Gruffydd built this ghost infested citadel in about 1200. At first he supported Prince Llywelyn but when it suited him he turned to help the Norman invaders, but by 1282 Dinas Bran was an important base of Welsh resistance. The strategic value of this high hill above the river valley suggests that a Dinas (the Welsh word for a city or a settlement) must have been here many years before the Normans marched into Wales, and before Madog replaced the earlier fortifications with the present 'castell'. Leland called it a 'battered ruin', and when Wordsworth saw it he described it as,

Relic of Kings, wreck of forgotten wars,
To the winds abandoned and the prying stars.

Even before the days of Llangollen's now famous musical festival the town became known for its two ladies who lived at the lovely timbered Plas Newydd on the outskirts of the town. The 'Ladies of Llangollen', the Hon Sarah Ponsonby and Lady Eleanor Butler were eccentric Irish ladies who came here from Ireland in 1779. They were ladies of culture who entertained famous people from all parts of Britain, among them were the Duke of Wellington and Sir Walter Scott who upset the two ladies when he described their lovely house as 'a low-roofed cottage'. He was never invited there again. Plas Newydd, open to the public, displays an interesting collection of carved woodwork collected by the two ladies.

Not far away from Llangollen is another house with memories of less genteel times. At a spot known as 'Worlds End' is Plas yr Eglwyseg, a Tudor house standing on the site of the hunting lodge of the bold young Prince Cadwgan of Powys. To this hidden lodge the infatuated Cadwgan brought (and she was not unwilling) the lady Nest, wife of Gerald de Windsor, the Lord of Pembroke Castle. This abduction plunged Wales into war, and the reckless Welsh prince was forced to flee to Ireland. He would have lived longer had he stayed there, for years afterwards he was slain by De Windsor during a battle in which they fought on the same side. A tablet in the present house records the history.

There is a lot to see and interest the visitor to Llangollen. Near the medieval bridge is a building where you can still see fabrics being woven, and woollen goods are displayed and sold. From this house of the Llangollen Weavers there is pleasant walk along a terrace alongside the Dee. Above the north side of the town is the tree-shaded canal on which you can enjoy trips in horse drawn barges, and on the wharf is the Canal Museum.

After crossing the Dee the A542 climbs through a wooded valley and soon, on the right below the road, you will see the ruins of Valle Crucis Abbey. Its name was probably more acceptable to its occupants learned in the Latin tongue than to the Welsh who called it Glyn-y-Groes. Madog of Dinas Bran founded the abbey in 1202 for the Cistercians who must have been delighted with their home near the Eglwyseg stream which they no doubt diverted to feed their fishponds. Was Owain Glyndwr buried here? It is impossible to be certain, but records say that he was last seen here by the abbot who, when Owain bade him a good morning, commenting that he was about unduly early, the abbot replied, 'nay my lord Owain, it is you who are up too early – a hundred years too early'.

A few miles above the abbey the road makes a great horseshoe bend around the outlying spurs of the Llantysilio Mountain. Soon after reaching its junction with the A5104 and A525 our route passes the ancient encampment of Castell-y-Rhodwydd to enter the southern entrance of the Vale of Clwyd, a rich undulating area well irrigated by the watershed of the surrounding hills.

The two principal towns in the Vale are Ruthin and Denbigh. It was at Ruthin in 1400 that the long smouldering discontent of the Welsh burst into flame. Led by Owain Glyndwr, victim of the lying treachery of Lord Grey of Ruthin, they attacked the town on the eve of St Matthews Fair. They set the town on fire, but it was two years before Glyndwr was able to capture his enemy Grey and imprison him at Dolbadarn Castle in the Llanberis Pass. The Glyndwr rising convulsed Wales for 14 years, the Welsh leader marching his avenging armies throughout the length and breadth of the land.

Ruthin Castle, built by Edward I in 1281, withstood many attacks, only falling after a three month siege in 1646 when it was taken and demolished by Cromwell. Enough of it remains to make it worthwhile visiting, and now, as the Ruthin Castle Hotel, its walls resound to the gay sounds of bogus medieval banquets and not to the clash of arms. Leaflets invite you to 'quaff wine from pewter goblets; eat nourishing medieval dishes with a dagger, be pampered by the ladies of the court, and listen to beautiful harp music in the candle-lit Banquet Hall.' A less expensive way of savouring the atmosphere of the past is by visiting Ruthin on a Wednesday morning in July or August. Each Wednesday the shopkeepers and people of the town, dressed in colourful medieval costume, sell their goods and display their skill in weaving, spinning and other ancient crafts in St Peter's Square. It is a colourful scene, and if you feel hungry the chef of Myddleton Arms Hotel will tempt you with a cut from the piglet he is roasting on a spit in front of the hotel, or if you would like to taste something different he will suggest you have a portion of his dish of the day – his 'Dragon pie'.

George Borrow thought it 'a dull town, but it possessed plenty of interest for me', an interest he showed by describing his guided tour of the castle. He wrote,

She (his guide) showed us dark passages, a gloomy compartment in which Welsh kings and great people had been occasionally con-fined; that strange memorial of the good old times, a drowning pit, and a large prison room, in the middle of which stood a singular looking column, scrawled with odd characters, which had of yore been used for a whipping post, another reminder of the good old baronial times, so dear to romance readers and minds of sensibility.

Practically every street in the town has one or more buildings of interest. In St Peter's Square is the 14th century Courthouse and place of execution. Next to the 18th century Castle Hotel is the unique multidor-mered facade of the 16th century Myddleton Arms, and on the opposite side of the square is a block of stone, Maen Huail, which is supposed to have been used as an improvised block for beheading one who was King Arthur's rival for the hand of a lady. Stryd-y-Castell (Castle Street) has the picturesque Judge's residence of Nantclwyd House, and in Well Street No. 2 dates from the 15th century, distinguished by being one of the few houses that survived when the town was burnt by Glyndwr in 1400. Another house in Well Street is proud to have been where the Welsh National Anthem was first printed. Apart from containing so many buildings of the medieval period the town has interesting exam-ples of Georgian and Regency architecture. Ruthin is perhaps the most

Market Day in St. Peter's Square, Ruthin. Between the clock tower and the Castle Hotel is the unusual multi-dormered roof of the Myddleton Arms.

This 14th-century building, now a bank, was once Ruthin's Courthouse and place of execution.

completely interesting town in Wales, and a walk around its narrow streets will convince you of this.

As Denbigh is neared the Clwyd Valley widens to allow an easy entry into the town. Like so many other towns in the Welsh Marches Denbigh grew around the castle, becoming important when Edward I granted its first Charter. Overlooking the Vale of Clwyd it lives up to Defoe's description as being 'a most pleasant, fruitful popular and delicious vale, full of villages and towns, the fields shining with corn, just ready for the reaper, the meadows green and flowery'. Lanes from the High Street lead to Castle Hill, a viewpoint from where the prospect of the Clwydian hills rising gently above the valley is peaceful, so that one forgets the turmoil and noise of yesterdays battles.

The streets are lined with buildings of variety in shape and colour; one, the County Hall, was originally built in 1572 by the Earl of Leicester, and not far away is a church he began to build which was to replace St Asaph's Cathedral. It was never completed so today it is known as 'Leicester's Folly'. There are several interesting old inns and one of them, The Bull, was busy in coaching days. Today it is more interesting inside than out, having a magnificent oak staircase with carvings reminding one of the days when fine gloves were made in Denbigh. A friary was founded here in the 13th century by Sir John Salesbury, or Salusbury, a knight said to have had two thumbs on each hand. It is said that he was responsible for giving the town its name. This happened when the brave knight killed a dragon which lived in a cliff cave below the castle. After a long fight he cut off the creature's head, and when he showed it to the people they shouted 'DIM BYCH', which is said (although this interpretation is dubious) to mean 'no more dragon', so the town was called Dimbych – which became corrupted to Denbigh. Sir John, so it is claimed, also enhanced his reputation by stunning a lion with his fist in the Tower of London. Space does not permit writing about everything of interest in Denbigh, but a booklet issued by the County Planning Department will help the visitor.

The castle was not a lucky home for its owners; the Norman Lord De Lacy, who initiated its building, lost his son who fell into a deep well and was drowned before he could be pulled out. Hugh Despenser, the unpopular favourite of Edward II was hanged, then Jasper Tudor marched south to suffer defeat at Mortimer's Cross. Another custodian, Robert Dudley, the Earl of Leicester, was not successful in furthering his ambitions by marriage to his queen. After his defeat near Chester Charles I sought shelter within the castle walls, but left as soon as he heard that his enemies were marching on the town.

Denbigh is another excellent tourist centre. The A543 after crossing a well defined section of Offa's Dyke near Bodfari reaches Caerwys where the Romans built their strongest fort between Caerleon and Chester.

Rhuddlan. On the site of an earlier Welsh castle the later Norman fortress of Edward I overlooks a marshland where a Welsh force was slaughtered by the Mercian army of King Offa in 798.

The land around served as battle fields since the Roman occupation. In the 11th century Rhys-ap-Tewdr, Prince of South Wales, came to help Gruffydd-ap-Cynan win the crown of North Wales. Records confirm that it was here that Gruffydd organised the first Eisteddfod to be held in Wales. Caerwys also boasts that the American, William Penn, based the layout of Philadelphia on the street plan of this little Welsh town.

Further north, on the bank of the River Elwy, is St Asaph where St Cynderyn founded a monastic cell which was replaced in later years by a small cathedral. There are varied opinions of this little 'cathedral city'. Defoe who travelled extensively in Wales, thought it 'but a poor town and ill-built. The outspoken Dr Johnson considered that 'the cathedral, although not large, has something of dignity and grandeur'. It is the smallest in Wales and England but has some points of interest. The roof was painted and gilded in 1967 to commemorate the investiture at Caernarfon Castle of the Prince of Wales, and there are memorials to past bishops. There is one to Richard Davies who translated the New Testament into Welsh; to William Morgan who translated the Bible into Welsh during the reign of Elizabeth I, and a revised version of this was started by Richard Parry in 1604. Before these were written the cathedral contained a copy of the 1579 'Breeches Bible', so called by the passage describing the moment when Adam and Eve discovered their naked-ness. It says,

> The eyes of both of them were opened . . . and they sewed figge-leaves together and made themselves breeches.

We stop next at Rhuddlan where a ruined castle overlooks the marshland where Offa and his Mercian army slaughtered the Welsh in 798. This terrible carnage is remembered by the plaintive lament of 'Morfa Rhuddlan'. An early Welsh castle, built by Llywelyn-ap-Seisyllt, was replaced by the one whose ruins we see today. Edward I, wishing to establish his complete sovereignty, summoned Welsh princes and leaders here to sign the hated 'Statute of Rhuddlan' in 1284. A stone building not far from the castle has a tablet on a wall claiming that it was the Parliament House of King Edward I, and used by the Norman king for the signing of the Treaty. It was at Rhuddlan Castle that Edward is said to have received news that his son had been born at Caernarfon. The Dee-side fortress was attacked many times, becoming indefensible after its walls had been torn apart by Civil War cannons.

Dyserth, a short distance to the east, is overlooked by the site of a castle built by Henry II in 1241. It had a short life for 22 years later it was destroyed by Llywelyn the Last. Near the village is a 60 feet high waterfall, seen at its best after a spell of continuous rain. If you are interested in antique armour and furniture a visit to nearby 17th century

A tablet on the wall of this ancient stone building claims that Edward I held a parliament at Rhuddlan in 1283.

Bodrhyddan Hall will be enjoyable. Our journey through this land of the Lords Marchers ends at Prestatyn, a town near the end of Offa's Dyke which stops just short of the coast after stretching 167 miles from the mouth of the River Wye at Chepstow in Gwent.

Our ancestors lived here some 6,000 years ago, their existence being proved by the discovery of their skeletons and primitive tools on the site of a Stone Age village above Prestatyn. When the old Celtic saints reached here they tore down the sacrificial altar stone and in the centre of the pagan stone circle, which became a sanctified 'llan', a Christian church was built. It was not easy for the people to forget the old ways, and the native warriors with folk-memories of previous pagan ways and superstitions sharpened the blades of their weapons on the rim of the font – believing that their swords and daggers would be endowed with a special virtue and power.

Prestatyn is one of several similar seaside holiday towns along the coast of North Wales. Linked by holiday camps and over-crowded caravan sites they form a coastal playground for the people of the North of England and the Midlands.

Along the Dee Estuary to Chester

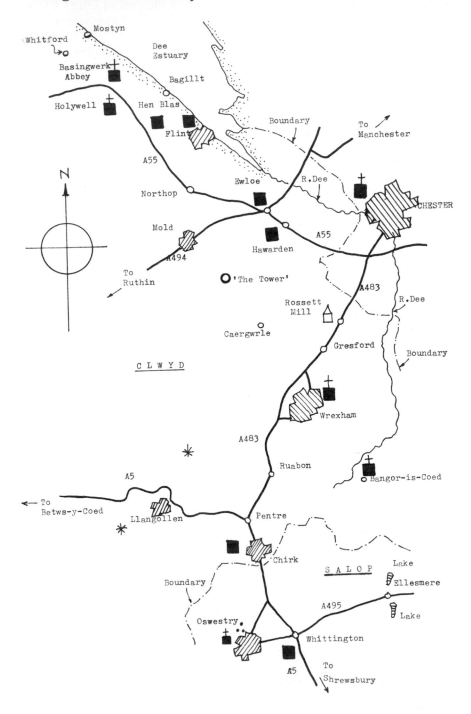

CHAPTER FOURTEEN

Along the Dee Estuary to Chester

Our final journey takes us along the southern coast of the Dee Estuary to Chester. Not far south of the mouth of the estuary is Mostyn which was once an important port of embarkation for ships carrying coal and merchandise to Ireland. Mostyn and a 15th century mansion are named after that of a family who helped the Earl of Richmond defeat Richard III at Bosworth. When the young earl was a guest at Mostyn Hall he was nearly captured by the king's soldiers, being forced to leave his dinner and leap through a window. When questioned about the extra dinner plate and cutlery the quick-witted host persuaded the king's officers that it was an old family custom to always lay a place for any unexpected guest. His invitation for them to dine with him allowed the young earl time to escape. Nearby is Whitford where, until it was destroyed by fire in 1922, was another mansion, the birthplace of Thomas Pennant (1726–1778) the traveller and historian. Whitford is also known to have the tallest Celtic cross in Wales, one which dates from the 10th century.

A few miles further along the A548 are the remains of Basingwerk Abbey, founded in 1131 for the monks of the Savigny order who 16 years after they came here amalgamated with the Cistercians. This amalgamation may not have been welcomed by the Cistercians who preferred to lead an austere and simple life, but it was not long before they came to accept a richer and more comfortable way of living. It is recorded that before the Dissolution the abbey guests were numerous, and very anxious to join the well-fed bretheren at their refectory tables which were heavily laden with rich foods and fine wines from French and Spanish vineyards.

Just west of the ruins of Basingwerk Abbey is Holywell, the Welsh Treffynon. It was a known place in the 7th century, called Hali-well by the Saxons, and the home of a virgin named Wenefrede. So great was her beauty that many sought her hand in marriage. The most persistant of her many suitors was Prince Cradocus who, when she refused him, drew his sword and cut off her head. An old legend relates that,

> The severed head took its way down the hill and stopped near the church . . . . A spring of uncommon size burst from the place where the head rested. . . . Her blood spotted the stones, which, like the

The ruins of Basingwerk Abbey, originally founded in 1131 for monks of the order of Savigny.

Harwarden Castle, built in 1750, became one of the homes of Prime Minister W.E. Gladstone after his marriage to a Welsh heiress.

flowers of Adonis, annually commemorate the fact, by assuming colours unknown to them at other times.

The legend continues to tell of the miraculous resurrection of Wenefrede when her uncle, St Beuno,

> Took up the head, carried it to the corpse, and offering up his devotions, joined it nicely to the body, which instantly reunited. The place was visible only by a slender white line encircling the neck.

St Winifred (Wenefrede) lived for 15 years after her resurrection becoming the abbess of a convent near Llanrwst where she was buried in 650. No trace of the convent remains, but a stone engraved W I N may have been the headstone on her grave until she was re-buried in Shrewsbury Abbey.

Holywell became known as the 'Lourdes of Wales', and the holy well erected over the healing spring in the 15th century by the Countess of Darby (mother of Henry VII) has been the scene of many miraculous cures. Red moss grows on the stones at the bottom of the well, and this is considered by many to be the hair and blood of St Winifred whose statue is in a wall niche above the well. It is known that a lady named Winifred White was instantly cured of a serious complaint after bathing in the well on the 11th June 1908. Annual pilgrimages are still made to Holywell. A publication of 1820, by an unknown author, 'The Miracles of Wales', mentions the well and tells of,

> Hundreds of sick folk who have arrived on crutches, but who can run back home. On the stones of the well may be seen clearly the blood of Winefrede which fell when she was beheaded there.

Further south is Bagillt, sharing with Mostyn the facilities of a port and small industries by having blast furnaces and collieries. Bagillt never had a fine abbey or church of distinction, but between the A548 and A55 there once stood Hen Blas Castle. This was probably an early motte and bailey, but in 1244 the palisade which surrounded the motte may have been replaced by a strong wooden keep.

Flint has more to show, for between the town and the Dee stand the ruins of a castle built by Edward I in 1277. Before then the Normans may have made use of some primitive defences on Twt Hill near Rhuddlan. When Edward II recalled the exiled Piers Gaveston from exile in Ireland he entertained him at Flint, and his welcome and his bed-chamber was better and warmer than the dark cold dungeon used to incarcerate

Richard II after he surrendered to Bolingbroke in August 1399. According to Shakespeare the treacherous Bolingbroke at first welcomed the king, and,

> On both his knees did kiss King Richard's hand,
> And sends his allegiance and a true faith of heart.

At this time and for years afterwards Flint was a prosperous town, for before the Dee silted up ships carried lead ore mined from the Halkyn Mountains to ports across the sea. The Romans too have worked the mountains for the precious ore.

From Flint the A5119, after crossing the A55 near Northop, will bring you to Mold, a town whose roots began to grow in 430 when St Germanus, Bishop of Aukene, sent an army to help the Britons defeat the pagan Picts. The victory of the Britons was unusually bloodless, achieved when they made a simultaneous shout of 'ALLELUIA' making the pagan forces believe that larger forces than they expected were facing them, so they marched away. This was called the 'Alleluia Victory' and an obelisk was set up at Maes Garmon where this took place. The story of Mold continued when the Normans raised a castle motte on a hill now known as Bailey Hill, and until it was captured in 1144 by Owain Gwynedd it was impregnable. After its recapture it fell again to Prince Llywelyn Fawr in 1159, a date which marks his rise to power.

The ferocity of battles between the Welsh and Anglo-Normans is exemplified by what took place a few miles south of Mold at a spot marked on the map as 'The Tower'. Here, after capturing the mayor and some senior citizens of Chester who were attending a fair at Mold, a Welsh chieftain hanged them from hooks in the hall of the Tower. When a force of about 40 men came from Chester to exact revenge they found the tower deserted, but no sooner than they were all inside the Welsh closed and battened the entrance door; by a pre-arranged plan the Tower became a dreadful incinerator from which not one of the unfortunate men escaped.

Excavations near Mold have uncovered relics of early times. Acting on a persistent story that a ghostly horseman, clad in golden armour and a cloak, haunted a hill called Bryn-yr-Ellyllan, a burial cairn or mound on the hill was excavated in 1832. Inside the mound, dated from 900 to 600 BC, was found the skeleton of a Celtic chieftain covered by a ceremonial cape of leather decorated with designs in gold of Celtic origin. This remarkable relic can be seen in the British Museum, and a facsimile is in the National Museum of Wales at Cardiff.

Richard Wilson the 18th century landscape painter is buried at Mold, and near his grave lies that of Daniel Owen, the Welsh novelist who wrote about the unhappy lot of workers in the mining and other industries in the 19th century.

Mold has been an important point of junction for countless years; in Roman times their military highway from Chester (Castra Deva) to the fort of Canovium near the head of the Conway Valley ran close to Mold. A short way east is Buckley, a town spread along both sides of the A549 road to Chester. The Romans found the quality of the clay here to be very suitable for manufacturing their earthenware, and in the 18th century Buckley clay was used for making bricks. Evidence of Roman occupation was confirmed in 1606 when an excavation at Caergwrle uncovered an 18 feet length of a well preserved hypocaust; the tiles used in its construction being stamped LEGIO XX. Another period of occupation was again confirmed when a 6th century bowl made of black oak and decorated with designs in gold was found. The bowl, known as 'the Caergwrle Bowl', is in the Welsh National Museum at Cardiff.

A road runs northwards over Buckley Mountain to Ewloe where are the ruins of a castle taken from the Normans by Owain Gwynedd in 1146. Soon after the A55 from Ewloe crosses a railway you will reach Hawarden, a place recorded in the Domesday Book as 'Haordine', but now its name is pronounced as Harden. To control the approaches from North Wales the invaders hurriedly set up a fortress of earthworks and timber, but this was soon destroyed by the Welsh, leaving only the charred remains of a palisade until Edward I built there a stone castle. This in turn was battered by the Welsh, but some of the walls stood until an attack during the Civil War left it a complete ruin.

The map indicates two castles, the one we have just read about is marked CASTLE (ruins of) the second one is marked HAWARDEN CASTLE which was built in 1750. The latter castle, by marriage, came into the ownership of Prime Minister W.E. Gladstone when he married the Welsh heiress, Catherine Glynne in 1839. Gladstone loved this part of Wales, particularly the mountain and coastal region between Conway and Llanfairfechan. The castle-mansion of Hawarden became his principal home and he lived there for 60 years until his death in 1898. Although he is entombed in Westminster Abbey there are memorials to William and Catherine in the local church, and nearby St Deniol's Library, which he founded, is another memorial to 'the Grand Old Man', four times Prime Minister of Britain.

Chester, by way of Saltney, is only a short distance away, but before exploring this ancient and historic city which will end our exploration of the Welsh Marches and Borderlands, and this book, we will return to the junction of the A5 with the A483 just north of Chirk at a point where the A483 crosses the Vale of Llangollen and the River Dee at Newbridge.

If, before proceeding northwards towards Wrexham, you would like to explore an area where the scenery is less rugged and of quite a

*The tower of St. Giles at Wrexham is another of the 'Seven Wonders of Wales'.
Elihugh Yale, founder of the American university, is entombed near the foot of
the tower.*

different character to that of Wales, turn south and take the A5 road signposted to Shrewsbury. In no time at all you will reach the small village of Whittington where the twin towers of a gateway to a moated castle cast their shadow over the highway. Cross the short stone causeway which bridges the moat, and after passing through the gateway you will be standing in the courtyard of a castle which once belonged to the Lord Marcher Fulke FitzWarine who dominated this part of the borderland. From here the A49 leads to Ellesmere which takes its name from the Mere (lake) just east of the town. The mansion of Otely overlooks the lake, replacing in importance a castle built by Roger de Montgomery. When Llywelyn Fawr married Joan, daughter of King John, he received the castle as part of his bride's dowry, but now only the site of it remains. South of Ellesmere are several smaller lakes, accounting for the surrounding countryside being known as 'Shropshire's Little Lake District'.

Ruabon, Rhubon, or if these names are not acceptable to a Nationalistic Welshman, Rhiwabon, is only interesting today as a manufacturing centre for well known brands of brick and tile, and that a mansion here was the seat of Baron Watcyn Williams Wynn, a man prominent in the 19th century social life of Wales.

In a few miles a turning on the right leads to Wrexham, a town certain to be visited by American visitors wishing to pay homage to a fellow-countryman who founded Yale University. Elihugh Yale came with his parents from America to live in Wales at the age of four, and although he travelled a great deal he lived most of his life in Wales until his death in 1721 at the age of 72. When the Yale University was being designed he persuaded the architect to design one of its towers as an exact replica of the tower of Wrexham Church – the tower which is listed among 'the Seven Wonders of Wales'. The epitaph on his tomb, which was restored by Yale University in 1874, does not reveal that Elihugh was sometimes a hard and bad tempered man, a fact which must have been true if the story is correct that he once hanged a groom for riding his horse, exercising it for three days without his permission. The inscription on the tomb reads,

> Born in America, Europe bred,
> In Africa travelled, in Asia wed,
> Where long he lived and thrived; In London dead,
> Much good, some ill he did: so hope's all even,
> And that his soul thro' mercy's gone to Heaven.
> You that survive and read this tale, take care
> For this most certain exit to prepare;
> Where blest in peace, the actions of the just
> Smell sweet and blossom in the dust.

The moated castle of Whittington, the home of Fulk FitzWarine, the Marcher Lord who ruled this part of the borderland.

At Rossett, on the bank of the Alyn river, the 14th-century cornmill is being restored.

This epitaph suggests that in his lifetime 'all was not sweetness and light', and it was hoped that his passage into the hereafter was made easy – and it certainly ends with a warning. Another character of very uncertain temper born here was the notorious 'Hanging Judge' Jeffreys. He was appointed Chief Justice at Chester in 1680.

Being close to the Welsh border the ownership of Wrexham was often contested. When Offa built his dyke he made certain that the town was in his Mercian kingdom, but in time the Welsh pushed the Saxon invader back to the English side of the Dee. The church, dedicated to St Giles, with such a fine high tower is a landmark for miles around.

This was an area of Wales which suffered the scourge of paganism, and Bangor-is-Coed, south-east of Wrexham, was a place that suffered more than most. A monastery established here in the 2nd century – although no traces of it remain – was a building large enough to accommodate 2,000 monks. King Ethelfrith of Northumbria required the monks to pray for his victory in a battle he was just about to mount against the Welsh. When the monks refused to pray for a pagan victory the king slaughtered 1,000 of them. The 1,000 who escaped fled across North Wales to Bardsey Isle which afterwards became known as 'the Isle of a Thousand Saints'.

Continuing our way to Chester we come to Gresford, which the Welsh called Groesfford. This coal mining town is known for two things – its magnificent Perpendicular church whose peal of bells are included in the 'Seven Wonders of Wales', and also for a terrible mining disaster when an explosion and fire killed 261 mineworkers in September 1934. Further north is the village of Rossett where the flow of the River Alyn once turned the wheel of a very picturesque 14th century cornmill. The wheel, probably a replacement, and machinery was still working up to 1961. It is understood that the old mill is to be restored.

Chester

Our exploration of the Welsh Marches and Borderlands ends at Chester, a city which is considered as 'the Jewel of the North West of England, and the county town of Cheshire. It is the only completely walled town in Britain, its history starting in AD 48 as the Roman Castra Deva, or Castrum Legionis. It was then the headquarters of one of the three Roman legions in Britain and garrisoned by a force of 13,000 men. Proof of its importance exists in the Roman stonework of cellar walls beneath the modern streets, and foundations of military buildings, baths, and an amphitheatre can still be seen. The wide streets of the town overlay many which were laid down by Roman engineers.

When the Romans left Britain, despite Chester being a comfortable

Alongside the medieval wall of the city of Chester the stones and columns of the Romans give proof of their long occupation of Castra Deva.

The Cross and Rows at the junction of the Roman streets of Via Principalis *and* Via Decumana.

and well fortressed place in which to live, the Anglo-Roman inhabitants, as happened in other Roman settlements, neglected the defences to such a degree that subsequent foreign invaders had little difficulty in taking the former Roman city. Ethelfrith, who slaughtered the monks of Bangor-is-Coed, replaced the pagan Roman temples with those to honour his particular heathen gods, then about 230 years later the Mercian kings occupied Chester.

When the Normans came they found the resistance of the Welsh and northern people much tougher than any they met in the south, so it was several years before they were able to establish a base to make forays into the Marches of Wales. It was the last town in England to submit to the Marcher Lords of the Conqueror.

It was in the Middle Ages that Chester began to develop into the interesting town we see today, with medieval buildings rising from the Roman foundations of yesteryear, following the lines of streets which were walked by the Roman legions 2,000 years ago. In 1644, besieged by Cromwell's forces, the town held out for almost two years before surrendering, but when a plague broke out in 1648 the pestilence, showing no respect or favour, attacked the supporters of Crown and Parliament.

In happy and less happy circumstances kings and nobles came to Chester. Three years after landing at Hastings William the Conqueror came, mocking the fact that Edgar, the first Saxon king of a united England, was crowned there by St Dunstan. Earl Leofric and his Lady Godiva were also visitors, and Richard II came there in gratitude to review the 2,000 archers the city provided for his army, but he was less pleased when he was later imprisoned for a time in Chester Castle. Charles I must have had mixed feeling after watching the defeat of his army from a tower on the city walls. The latest royal association with the historic city is happier, for Prince Charles is not only the Prince of Wales but also the Earl of Chester.

Space does not allow a detailed description of this most interesting of all the border towns – this must be left to many of the excellent Guide Books which are available, but if the visit is short a walk along The Rows or the ancient city walls will whet the appetite for a future and longer visit.

From the Rows can be seen many of the finest medieval timbered buildings, most of them being houses which now are shops and business premises. The Rows are a double-decker tier of shops at ground and first floor levels. The upper shops front on to balconies overlooking the streets below, offering a safe and pleasant pedestrian way for shoppers above the busy traffic filled streets. An early and quaint description of the Rows tells us of,

Sketch Map of Chester Town Centre

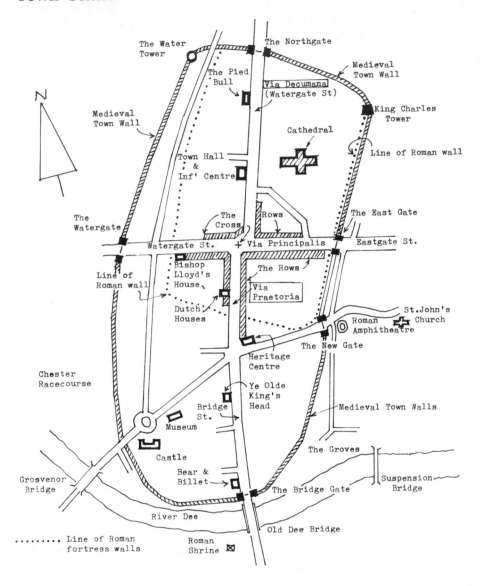

The Water Tower

The Northgate

Medieval Town Wall

The Pied Bull

Via Decumana (Watergate St)

King Charles Tower

Medieval Town Wall

Cathedral

Line of Roman wall

Town Hall & Inf' Centre

The Watergate

The Cross

Rows

The East Gate

Watergate St.

Via Principalis

Eastgate St.

Line of Roman wall

Bishop Lloyd's House

The Rows

Via Praetoria

St.John's Church

Dutch Houses

Roman Amphitheatre

The New Gate

Heritage Centre

Chester Racecourse

Ye Olde King's Head

Bridge St.

Medieval Town Walls

Museum

Castle

The Groves

Grosvenor Bridge

Bear & Billet

The Bridge Gate

Suspension Bridge

River Dee

Old Dee Bridge

········ Line of Roman fortress walls

Roman Shrine ⊠

. . . galleries wherein passengers go dry without coming into the streets, having shops on both sides and underneath, the fashion thereof is somewhat hard to conceive. (*suggesting that a visit is necessary to appreciate the planning arrangement*) It is therefore worth their pains, who have money and leisure, to make their own eyes the expounders of the manner thereof . . .

To mention but a few of the historic buildings which can be seen from the Rows and in adjoining streets, No. 23 The Row is built above cellars of the Roman period; below No. 39 can be seen the hypocaust of a Roman bath. In Lower Bridge Street the Pied Bull claims to be Chester's oldest hostelry, but many others compete in age and interest, such as the King's Head and Ye Olde Boot Inn in Eastgate Street. In well preserved Watergate Street you can see the richly carved facade of Bishop Lloyd's house, and near it is the Old Custom House Inn of 1637. If you care to browse among interesting books, No. 12 Bridge Street is the place to go, and below this shop you can see a well restored medieval crypt. Another, and effortless way of obtaining an introduction to Chester is to visit the Heritage Centre at the corner of Bridge Street and Pepper Street. There you can enjoy an audio-visual film show which will guide you through the city and inform you of what to see.

Other ancient relics and buildings of far off days can be seen on a brief walk along the city walls. These walls, replacing the Roman ramparts, are mainly medieval but here and there Roman stonework can be identified. We can climb steps to enter King Charles's Tower from where he watched the battle of Rowton Moor. Another section of the wall nearly touches the Lady Chapel of Chester Cathedral. The cathedral is dedicated to St Werburg, but excellent guide books are available for those who wish to learn more about the founding and the history of this beautiful building.

One of the gate-entrances in the city wall, opened in 1938, is properly called the Newgate. Near this modern gateway is an extensive section of Roman walling marking the south-east corner of their fortress. Near this, only discovered and excavated in 1929, is a large part of their amphitheatre, the largest yet discovered in Britain. This eliptical shaped Roman arena is conveniently near to the Grosvenor House Museum which has a varied and rich collection of Roman and medieval artefacts which tell the story of the history of Chester. There are inscribed and sculptured stones, one honouring Julius Agricola, the most famous of Britain's Roman Governors. You can study models of the Rows as they had been, and other models show the layout of the city from Roman to modern days.

The exploration of this beautiful city, whether by way of the ancient streets or 'walking the walls' can be very exhausting, so pleasant

The long history of the city of Chester is reflected by its buildings, the timber-framed structures of medieval times rising above the foundations of the Roman city of Deva.

relaxation is possible by taking a trip on the Dee by motor-launch, or even aboard a horse-drawn barge. The river landing stages are easy to find; after passing through the Newgate at the end of Pepper Street, with the site of the Roman amphitheatre on your left, walk down Souter's Lane. At the bottom of the Lane you will reach The Groves where landing stages line the Dee on both sides of a graceful suspension bridge. One interesting river trip is to Eaton Hall and its lovely gardens.

There are several interesting places within easy reach of Chester; Eaton Hall, already mentioned, can also be reached by road. Visit Malpas, one of the prettiest village in Cheshire. If you wish to try your hand at treasure-hunting go to Beeston Castle where a 360 feet deep well is said to contain treasure which Richard II had thrown down the well to keep it out of Bolingbroke's grasping hands. The well has been explored but up to now no treasure has been pulled out of it.

Our long journey through the historic English-Welsh Marches ends at Chester, a city, in all ways remarkable and one to which it is difficult to do justice.

Index

PERSONS